BEING AN OLDER WOMAN

ଓ ✦ ଓ

A Study in the
Social Production
of Identity

Everyday Communication: Case Studies of Behavior in Context
Wendy Leeds-Hurwitz & Stuart J. Sigman, Series Editors

BEING AN OLDER WOMAN

ॐ ◆ ೞ

A Study in the
Social Production
of Identity

Isabella Paoletti
Perugia, Italy

 LAWRENCE ERLBAUM ASSOCIATES, PUBLISHERS
1998 Mahwah, New Jersey   London

Lawrence Erlbaum Associates, Inc., Publishers
10 Industrial Avenue
Mahwah, New Jersey 07430

Library of Congress Cataloging-in-Publication-Data

Paoletti, Isabella
Being an older woman : a study in the social production of
identity / Isabella Paoletti.
        p. cm.
    Includes bibliographical references and indexes.
    ISBN 0-8058-2120-1 (cloth). — ISBN 0-8058-2121-X
(pbk.)
    1. Aged women—Psychology. 2. Day care centers for
the aged—Psychological aspects. 3. Women—Identity
I. Title.
    HQ1061.P325   1998
    305.26—dc21   97-25829
                                                  CIP

Books published by Lawrence Erlbaum Associates are printed
on acid-free paper, and their bindings are chosen for strength
and durability.

Printed in the United States of America
10 9 8 7 6 5 4 3 2 1

For Silva and Carolyn

Contents

Editors' Preface

Isabella Paoletti studies a universal phenomenon in *Being an Older Woman: A Study in the Social Production of Identity*—the identities available to the elderly in society. She does so by examining a particular site for the production of age identity: the meetings of a group of Italian women who participated in The European Older Women's Project. In doing this, she reveals that age identity is salient in contexts of interaction, and that this salience ebbs and flows depending on the situations and tasks in which participants find themselves involved. In this manner, being an older woman is an interactional accomplishment, but a sometimes one. That is, while age is always a physical fact, only sometimes does it become a socially relevant component of identity within interaction.

Paoletti employs an ethnomethodological framework to make sense of data collected through participant observation and videorecording. Focusing on the women in Perugia who took part in the European Older Women's Project and participated in a variety of activities at the local level (radio programs, theater and singing workshops) as well as international conferences and exchange visits, the data provide insights into the production of elderly identity by the women themselves and by others (e.g., men, civic leaders, etc.) with whom they come into contact.

As one might expect, the identity of the elderly is problematic. On the one hand, there are stereotypes of how the elderly do and should behave—stereotypes which some of the women refuse to accept. On the other hand, because the European Project and the local Perugia project were targeted to the elderly, there are strategic moments when the participants feel obliged to invoke the category. In this manner, this study makes visible the rhetorical dimensions of assuming an elderly identity. In addition, being elderly is revealed as only a facet of identity, as Paoletti clearly shows the difficulties that the women (as women) have when they must rely upon the beneficence of municipal employees and association presidents—nearly all of whom are male. Finally, what is especially valuable about the study is that it shows women attempting to remain (or become) active in their later years, women whose focus of attention has changed from home to community, and the difficulties that arise when they go against community expectations.

Being an Older Woman is the first book-length treatment to have emerged from the European Older Women's Project. For this reason, and for the fact that it sheds light on an important dimension of communication and context, we are pleased to welcome Isabella Paoletti's work into the "Everyday Communication" series.

Wendy Leeds-Hurwitz
Stuart J. Sigman

Prologue

Carrying out this research and being part of the European Older Women's Action Project have been exciting and fruitful ventures for me. I learned a lot about my own aging and I started to see ageism in my own behavior. In particular, it has been research as an integral part of a social intervention.

The European Older Women's Action Project (1991–1994) was intended to link older women's groups across Europe. This research was part of the project's initiatives since the beginning. A pilot research project was carried out in 1991–1992 (Paoletti, 1997c), as an action research project (Lomax, 1989; McNiff, 1988). The data gathering, through interviews, was aimed at involving older women in a reflection on their condition, and also at stimulating proposals and initiatives to be developed in two Senior Citizen Centers. Two sets of interviews were carried out in the Centers, located in two small towns bordering Perugia.

From the analysis of the pilot study, the great differences in older women's perceived identities were apparent: It seemed evident that "being an older women" could describe antithetical practices and discourses (Kamler, 1995; Smith, 1990). For example, Caterina and Carmen apparently live in a similar situation, insofar as they are both widows who live alone, but they describe their conditions very differently; Caterina appears to have given up (transcript conventions are reported in Appendix A):

> **Caterina:** I'm not interested in much else because I'm on my own and I ask the Lord to grant me a little good health to keep going a little longer, to see my grandchild grow up and that's all, and after that I'm not asking for anything else at this point. (Group A, 5/9/91)

At the other extreme, Carmen wants to enjoy her life:

> **Carmen:** I've got to the point that, I can say I'm younger now than when I was 40, when I wasn't yet 40 I went through the pains of Purgatory ... now, I go out dancing, and I sing, I come here to the Center. (Group A, 5/9/91)

These descriptions project very different life perspectives from the women involved, with evident consequences for the quality of their lives.

The relevance of gender differences in the use of the Senior Citizen Centers emerged strongly from the analysis of the pilot study as well. The women started to come regularly to the Center only after activities specifically designed for them were introduced. The Center was previously seen by the women as a "male space." Moreover, it emerged that the women generally had a restricted space of action, compared to men: They were often confined at home, although they might be in good health and have a positive financial situation (Paoletti, 1996). Many women identified the Senior Citizen Center as *the place* outside their house, that is, the only place where they could go outside their house. Diana, speaking about the Center says:

> **Diana:**   my life changed from night to day, because up until two years ago
> (I would) always (stay) at home, but instead then I'm always, out
> of the house ... I feel better now, younger than I did 10 years ago.
> (Group A, 4/30/91)

As a result of the pilot research, I became particularly interested in looking at institutional influence on older women's lives and perceived identities. The committee meetings of the European Action Project, as well as the theater workshops it sponsored, provided relevant data (a detailed list of the video data is reported in Appendix B). I was not interested in studying the meetings as such, that is, as structured or organized encounters (M. A. Atkinson, Cuff, & Lee, 1978; Boden, 1994; Cuff & Sharrock, 1985; Smith, 1990), but as institutionally organized spaces in which the women could produce new and different identities.

In October 1992 the data collection for the main study started with the systematic recording of all committee meetings of the Action Project and some of the theater workshops. I decided also to videotape the managing committee meetings of some Senior Citizen Centers in order to compare the data with a decision-making environment in which males were predominant. This also had a practical purpose. In fact, we had had various problems and difficulties in carrying out the workshops and other initiatives, in particular because of the resistance of some of the presidents of the Centers; therefore, we were interested in finding out if the problems were due to communication difficulties. We needed to verify the quality and quantity of information regarding the Action Project activities as reported by the women in the managing committees of the Senior Citizen Centers.

There was a symbiotic relationship between the research and the Action Project: the "reflexive space" created by the research provided stimuli and ideas to construct the Project and monitor it, while the Project allowed incredibly easy access to the recording of naturally occurring data relevant to older women's methods of identity production in relation to institutional interventions.

I was in the peculiar position of being an insider to the Project while at the same time an observer. This is documented in the videorecording of the committee meetings in which, on various occasions, I took part in the discussion. In one case, I was even the facilitator of the meeting, while I was videotaping it.

As an insider, I acquired fine and detailed background knowledge that was valuable for the analysis. It is difficult to imagine how a researcher could have gained such insight only as an observer, without actively participating in the planning, managing, and monitoring of the Project. And, as an observer, I could provide very useful feedback during the monitoring of the Project.

This double role poses epistemological and ethical questions of which I am very much aware: As a researcher, was I polluting the data by being an active member in the Action Project? As a member, was I exploiting my privileged observer position to influence the situation in such a way that could be damaging to the participants?

I believe that social research can hardly take place without affecting the very environment or subjects it is going to study; a researcher coming into a social environment necessarily contributes to its production. In this analysis, the researcher, myself, is considered one among the members; no special understanding of the situation is advocated. If contributing to the Action Project through the research activities is epistemologically unproblematic to my theoretical perspective, it still remains ethically accountable. To monitor this influence in a morally responsible way, being aware of the consequences of actions that were taken in relation to the research on the participants (for example, the effect of the release of information on specific people), was a constant concern. The influence of research on the social environment, though, can also be seen as a resource to be used effectively for all practical purposes, and I strived to achieve this.

Isabella Paoletti

Acknowledgments

I would like to thank all the women who took part in the project, participating with enthusiasm, and who put a lot of time, skills, passion and creativity in it. A special thanks to Maria Teresa Marziali, the Equal Opportunity officer in Perugia, and her colleague in London, Elisabeth Sclater, who made the project possible.

I am very grateful to colleagues and friends who offered feedback on this work, and in particular to Carolyn Baker for her useful comments and suggestions on the manuscript and for her constant support. I also would like to thank Wendy Leeds-Hurwitz and Stuart Sigman, for their patient work in the editing of the book.

1

Introduction

WHY STUDY OLDER WOMEN?

A healthy and active later life is not only an objective of great personal interest, but also one of social relevance. Women represent the great majority of older people and recent studies show that, although they live longer than men, they have more health and economic problems (Barer, 1994; Coopmans, Harrop, & Hermans-Huiskes, 1988; Ginn & Arber, 1992). It is important to find ways to highlight how they are, and can be, an active and productive part of their communities, and to promote policies that acknowledge and allow such an active role.

Ageism is widespread in Western societies (Arber & Ginn, 1991; Carver & Garza, 1984; Dreher, 1987; Stolnitz, 1994). Discrimination on the basis of age takes various forms, from the use of ageist language (Nuessel, 1982) to exclusion from employment (Levin & Levin, 1980; Uhlenberg, 1992), limitation of educational opportunities (Harold, 1992), and medical treatments (Adelman, Greene, Charon, & Friedmann, 1992; Beckingham & Watt, 1995; Hermanova, 1995), or segregation in senior-only housing arrangements (Nuessel, 1982).

Among older people, women suffer most from both ageism and sexism (Ginn, 1992; Ginn & Arber, 1991). In Italy, as well as throughout Europe, older women represent the majority of those with lowest income (Coopmans et al., 1988; Mengani & Gagliardi, 1993). Older women are more likely than men to live alone and experience loneliness and isolation (Harold, 1992; Mengani & Lamura, 1995; Moen, Dempster-McClain, & Williams, 1992), although it has been found that women are generally more likely than men to rely on informal support networks (Barer, 1994). Moreover, older women tend to have more health problems, in particular mobility and psychological problems (Coopmans et al., 1988). In Italy, data referring to prevailing diseases among men and women show noticeable gender differences, with frequency of arthritis and nervous disorders almost double among women (Mengani & Gagliardi, 1993).

Although older women represent the majority of older people, and have specific health, social, and economic problems, they are generally "invisible"

1

(Ginn & Arber, 1991; Harold, 1992) both in the gerontological literature and in service provision. It is particularly noticeable that in the UN report "Social Aspects and Countries Reviews of Population Aging: Europe and North America," older women are not even mentioned as a special risk group (Stolnitz, 1994). In general, policies are designed to refer to male elderly and rarely take into account older women's specific needs and preferences, as is illustrated in the case study presented in this volume.

THE SETTING

In order to provide background for the setting in which this study was developed, I describe the main phases of the creation and development of the Older Women's Action Project Perugia–Lewisham 1991–1994, that was designed to link older women's groups across Europe. From the beginning, I took part in the creation and management of the Action Project; the research reported in this book was carried out as part of the Action Project initiatives in Perugia.

Many descriptions of this project are possible; I provide here only the information necessary to understand the transcripts that are presented in the analysis (see also Paoletti, Sclater, & Kysow, 1993).

AIMS AND STRUCTURE
OF THE EUROPEAN ACTION PROJECT

In the winter of 1991, an officer of the Assessorato "Progetto Donna" (Equal Opportunity Unit) of the City of Perugia was contacted by a colleague from the Policy and Equalities Unit of the Borough of Lewishan in London. She was seeking partners to establish a project to link older women's groups across the European Community (EC) member states. The officer in Perugia was just planning activities that would increase women's use of the local Senior Citizen Centers, so she joined the initiative with much enthusiasm. That year, Ireland also took part in the project.

Lewishan is a very progressive borough "with a strong commitment to older people" (Cooper & Sydell, 1994). There are many older people's groups, and some of them are politically quite active. In particular, the Council established the Pensioners' Committee as a full committee of the Borough of Lewisham in 1987, in order to monitor the Borough's decisions affecting older people.

Perugia is a major town in the Umbria region, in the middle of Italy, with a population of about 150,000 inhabitants. Of these 16% were over 65 years old in 1986 (Segatori, Benvenuti, & Gristina, 1989). The first Senior Citizen

Center was created in Perugia in 1986; by 1991, 6 centers had already been established in the territory of Perugia; 5 more were created that year. At the time of this writing, there are 17 centers, community spaces where older people meet regularly for leisure and cultural activities. Users of these centers are generally working class or lower middle class, self-sufficient people, ranging in age from 50 to over 90 years. Older women, although they were the majority of the Senior Citizen Centers' members, were hardly using the centers when the project began.

On a snowy day in February 1991, the two officers and I had the first meeting in Perugia to design the structure of the Action Project. Aims of the 3-year project were: to make visible older women's contributions in the community, as well as to point out their specific needs and problems. We wrote, in the first funding request to the EC, in 1991:

> This is a joint women and pensioners equalities initiative, linking with other equalities structures in the EC. On that basis links have been made with equalities officers in Italy, and Age and Opportunity in Ireland to promote a method of working together and an action programme which will act as guides to good practice, and identify priorities for future action or service provision.

Funds were granted by the EC to cover the expenses of the international linkages of the project; for the initiatives carried out in each nation, funds had to be sought locally.

During the second year (1992–1993), older women's groups from Germany, Greece, and The Netherlands joined the project; in the last year (1993–1994), groups from Portugal and Denmark also joined. This was the result of a lot of work organizationally as well as individually: international meetings, exchange visits in various countries, exchange of information and materials among the women's groups, and correspondence among the women.

THE MEANING OF THE PROJECT
AT THE LOCAL LEVEL

The women participating in the Action Project in Perugia were mainly members of Senior Citizen Centers, community spaces located out of the city center in densely populated districts of the town and in small villages belonging to the Municipality of Perugia. The Centers are run by a managing committee elected by the members, meeting regularly to make decisions about initiatives and events organized by the Centers. The Centers were officially invited to take part in the Action Project, yet only 5 of 11 Centers participated. Women were generally scarcely represented on those governing committees, despite being the majority of members.

The available space varies across the Centers. Before the beginning of the European Action Project, the Centers were used mostly by men sitting at tables, playing cards. The initial resistance to using the Centers was clearly felt and expressed by many of the women I interviewed in the course of the Pilot Research Project in spring 1991 (Paoletti, 1997c). The following is a particularly vivid description of the uneasiness felt by one of the women entering a Center:

Researcher:	why do you think that, these initiatives aren't getting very far
Alba:	it's because there are very few of us and here, there isn't any space here the, the women won't come until the Municipality gives us the space, nothing will be resolved, because here, to walk through [in the middle of all these men
Researcher:	[no that's right, sure
Alba:	the first times I had to walk through the middle of all these men I nearly died, I wouldn't go in, I'd just stay outside
Researcher:	of course
Alba:	but when I'd go in I thought
Researcher:	of course
Alba:	I could feel
Researcher:	sure
Alba:	the cold run down my spine and really I'm not
Researcher:	it's not that you're a little girl

Singing workshops, run weekly by a music teacher, were effective in attracting the women. These workshops were funded by the Equal Opportunity Unit, as part of the Action Project initiatives, and were free of charge for the participants. Their implementation met with resistance in some cases, in one Center in particular, due to the lack of space. There was a long struggle to obtain the use of the only suitable room of the Center for 2 hours a week. The first singing workshops were carried out in a room full of men chatting and playing cards, a clearly inappropriate context.

The following year, theater workshops were introduced. In this case, again, although the workshops were open to all, they were attended mostly by women. The workshops were run by a professional actress who helped the participants create the plays they performed. The theater workshop was meant as a space for "creative reflection." The participants chose a topic and developed it through acting out episodes and situations; through various stages, they arrived at the creation of a theater script. Themes ranged from the reconstruction of their past experiences (as in such performances as "Christmas Tales," "The First Dancing Party," and "The Rice-Weeder") to their dreams and their present problems ("Little Stories of Everyday Life," "Tales of the Summer Market," "Grandmother's Fairy-

Tale," "From the Past to the Present," "What Will Become of Us?"). The theater workshops represented an institutionally organized space where women could act out feelings, thoughts, forms of behaviors, and abilities which are denied in their daily lives.

These workshops were a very effective means of bringing together the women. Many other initiatives were taken in connection with the Action Project: photography workshops; activities focused on solidarity across generations carried out in schools; public meetings organized to publicize the Project; workshops to help the women write poetry and stories and correspond with women in various European countries. Moreover, the women were interviewed by specialized magazines for the elderly; radio shows and TV programs sought their contributions; their singing and theater groups were invited to perform in geriatric homes, schools, and Senior Citizen Centers; and they took part in various international conferences. For these women, such experiences and activities have meant a great improvement in their lives and their health, as they have often testified, projecting new, different, and appealing life perspectives.

In October 1992, a committee was created, composed of women representatives only, from each Senior Center in Perugia and the Equal Opportunities officer who acted as a facilitator of the group. An average of 20 older women convened monthly in order to decide on any Action Project initiatives. Occasionally teachers, social workers, presidents of Senior Citizen Centers and men would participate in the meetings. I usually took part behind a video recorder. All names in the transcripts based on these meetings have been changed to insure confidentiality.

One of the main aims of the Action Project was to increase older women's participation in the decision-making processes in their own communities. At an institutional level, the management of the project meant a constant juggling for the organizers (the equal opportunity officer and me), between dragging the women into activities they would never have dreamt of participating in and relinquishing control as much as possible for the management of the activities themselves. It was a subtle and difficult task to stimulate the group, facilitate the committee meetings, and make proposals, gradually releasing control and leaving more and more space to the older women's autonomous initiatives.

In taking part in the Project, many women have learned, or more precisely, have become aware of, their skills in managing and organizing; consequently, their participation in decision making at various levels in their community has increased. Some of them have become members of the managing committees for their Senior Citizen Centers. The organization of the international meeting in Perugia, in November 1993, represented a special effort in this direction. Most of the women had never participated in a conference or seminar, yet they were directly involved in the choice of the topics of the workshops and in the structuring and planning of the meeting while they autonomously organized all the entertainment for the guests.

This international meeting occasioned the synthesis, discussion, and evaluation of the participants' experiences in the various countries in the course of the 3 years of the European Action Project of Older Women. A second aim of the meeting was to consolidate the network that had developed during the 3 years of the Action Project between older women in the different countries. It is a particular kind of network: It is a communication system not only at an institutional level, but at an interpersonal level. The women have exchanged experiences, photos, letters, recipes, poetry, songs—in short, pieces of their lives. We wanted to encourage this exchange, in order to establish a permanent European Network of Older Women.

THE DEVELOPMENT AT LOCAL
AND INTERNATIONAL LEVELS

The end of the Action Project marked the beginning of two important initiatives: the constitution of the Italian Association of Active/Older Women (AIDA) in Perugia and the creation of the Older Women Network (OWN) in Europe. Simultaneously, the Equal Opportunity Unit underwent a major restructuring.

The women's group in Perugia decided to constitute itself legally as a national association, AIDA. This is a significant outcome of the Project, considering the initial situation of the women and the emphasis that was given throughout the course of the project to women participating in the decision making and the managing of each activity, that is, their autonomous initiatives.

At the international meeting in Perugia, the idea of the creation of a network was launched. We had worked steadly on it since a meeting in Ireland in June 1995, during which the constitution of OWN (Europe) was discussed and finalized. Various older women's groups joined the network from eight European countries: Denmark, Germany, Greece, Ireland, Italy, The Netherlands, Portugal, Spain, and The United Kingdom. The first action of the Network was to represent the older women at the UN conference in Beijin. In fact, as stated in the draft constitution (1995), the network includes among its main objectives: "To affirm the rights and capacity of older women, through self-help, education and training social groups and political activity in order to contribute to policy development and change, at [a] local, national and international level" (Peretz & Soeur, 1996).

These positive outcomes were contrasted by a negative development in the Equal Opportunity Unit in Perugia. In December 1993, the Equal Oportunity Unit changed from an autonomous councilorship to one included in the Councillorship for Cultural Affairs, by an internal injunction; that meant a drastic reduction in the autonomous initiative of the Unit. The staff, composed of two officers and two secretaries in 1991, was halved in 1994; the officer presented a request to work part time, and the secretary was mostly involved in tasks related to the Cultural Affairs Unit; the Equal Opportunity Unit was vanishing.

The Unit's support to the older women's group was withdrawn. The financial investment of the Equal Opportunities Unit in the Action Project had steadly increased during the 3 years of the Project: it amounted to £5,090,000 in 1991, to £23,586,000 in 1992, and £37,040,000 in 1993. If those sums are not relevant in an absolute sense, they become significant when compared with the total budget of the Equal Opportunity Unit. For example, in 1993 the Unit was assigned £60,000,000, that is, the contribution to the Action Project represented more than half of the whole Unit budget. The theater and singing workshops were not funded by the Council in 1994–1995, so contributions had to be sought elsewhere; neither was the analysis phase of the research funded. The institutional and political reasons for this backlash to the success of the Action Project are complex, and it is not appropriate to discuss them exhaustively here; by my own understanding, the defunding was due to a political line of action that readily sustains initiatives on women's issues as part of electioneering, but then stops them when they start to become effective. Overall, the institutional fading of the Equal Opportunity Unit is indicative of the pervasive and constant resistance that had to be met in all the phases of its development.

SCOPE OF THE STUDY

This study looks at how older women's identities are socially constructed and, in particular, how they can be influenced by institutional intervention. Different perceptions of oneself as an older woman involve considerable differences in the definition of each person's possible spheres of action, and, therefore, in their life perspectives. The interest in the processes for the production of older women's identities is not only theoretical but also practical: The identification of discourses and social practices constituting the social image of the older person provides the tools needed to identify and deconstruct images producing marginalization.

Aging is a complex process (Barbato & Perse, 1992). I believe that in order to fight isolation and segregation of older people, in particular of older women, it is useful to resolve problems related to self-perception and marginalization. Such actions are as necessary as apparently more concrete intervention in the areas of finance and health.

I am particularly interested in looking at the influence of institutional setting on interactional processes that are identity-relevant. Studying the relationship between identities and settings can give insight into the processes of change, at personal as well as institutional levels. In order to specify the aims and scope of this study, at theoretical as well as practical levels, it is necessary to clarify the very notion of "identity."

THE SOCIAL CONSTRUCTION OF IDENTITY IN THE ETHNOMETHODOLOGICAL APPROACH

At a commonsense level, identity is thought of as an intrinsic property of the subject, the essential features that make a person oneself. The constructivist conception of identity contrasts radically with this ordinary notion (Ainlay & Redfoot, 1982; Gergen & Davis, 1985; Gergen & Gergen, 1983; Laws, 1995; Macellari, 1981; Shotter & Gergen, 1989). In particular, in the ethnomethodological perspective, identity is understood as an interactional accomplishment, negotiated and achieved by members in the course of ordinary events, as constitutive features of their social encounters (Garfinkel, 1967; Schenkein, 1978; Watson & Weinberg, 1982). Therefore, any social interaction can be studied for its processes of identity production. Conversational membership categorization activities are particularly salient features of identity work (Baker, 1984; Coupland, Coupland, Giles, & Henwood, 1991).

We adjust our talk with reference to our interlocutor: We tell a story differently if we talk to a child or to an adult, to a policeman or to a sister. Sacks referred to this property of talk as "recipient design" (in P. Atkinson, 1985).

Identification work is essential to social interaction; in producing and understanding utterances, members orient their talk to the specific identities of the participants. Identification work shapes both initiator planning of the talk as well as the receiver sense assembly, through the documentary method of interpretation. Identity attributions are part of the "presupposed knowledge of social structures" (Garfinkel, 1967) used by members to produce and to understand talk (Heritage, 1984). Therefore, any social encounter is potentially inspectable for its documenting of identity work.

Social interchange could hardly occur without reference to the context of interaction, and participants' identification work is a fundamental aspect of context. That is, reference to a known-in-common understanding of the specific motives or reasons for actions or accounts, works in part through inferences about identity attributions.

Both at the commonsense level, as well as in empirical studies, the notion of identity is vague though widely used. In ethnomethodological research, the concept of identity often refers to various dimensions of the subject. Empirical studies have focused on the interactional production and negotiation of personal characteristics (Paoletti, 1991, 1997a; Sacks, 1992); in particular, of social and institutional identities, implying membership in either specific social categories (Baker, 1983, 1984; Paoletti, 1995, 1997c; Paoletti, Giacalone, Perfetti, & Zuccherini, 1994; Sacks, 1992; Watson & Weinberg, 1982); or professional or institutional categories (Schenkein, 1978; ten Have, 1994; Wilson, 1991).

I do not intend to attempt to remedy the vagueness of the concept here; rather, I mean to use it. Identity is a concept in which personal, social, and institutional dimensions intertwine. In my study, I explore how these dimensions are related. Identity refers to the idiosyncratic characteristics of a person, as well as to socially and institutionally defined memberships. Different identities are constructed by members in reference to different occasions, relationships, settings, and so forth (Coupland, Coupland, & Grainger, 1991). We should perhaps not talk of identity but rather of identities that are context sensitive and relevant to the occasion.

According to ethnomethodology, identity production is a constant achievement, as well as a condition, of social interaction. Identity-relevant actions or discourses are subject to scrutiny, verification, support or contradiction by members, that is, they are subject to negotiation in the course of ordinary events.

Schenkein's study on identity negotiation describes the skillful play of projection and counterformulation among interlocutors in relation to what he called "abstract identities" (Schenkein, 1978). These are used as a background through which idiosyncratic, personally meaningful identities, relevant to the setting and to the occasion, can be negotiated in the course of the interaction. A systematic exploration of these members' conversational activities has been possible through the conceptualization of membership categories.

MEMBERSHIP CATETEGORIES
USED IN IDENTITY WORK

Membership categorization devices, as theorized by Sacks (1972), have been found to be central in collaborative production of identities by members (Baker, 1984; Coupland, Coupland, Giles, & Henwood, 1991; Jayyusi, 1984).

Sacks (1972) defined membership categorization devices as "any collection of membership categories" (p. 331) used to classify members of a society, such as gender, race, stage of life or family, and so on. Each categorization device is comprised of various related categories. For example, the "stage of life" categorization device would include categories such as child, adolescent, adult, elderly, and the like. According to Sacks (1992, Vol. 1), "a great deal of the knowledge that members of a society have about the society is stored in terms of these categories" (pp. 40–41).

At the core of ethnomethodology is an interest in studying how the stable features of social reality are produced and reproduced by members through their interaction. Membership categories seem to be the foundation blocks of the known-in-common social reality. In particular, Sacks (1992) pointed out the stable character of the knowledge stored in these categories; they are shown to be quite resistant to change, "protected against induction" (Vol. 1, p. 196). That is, if we associate a particular attribution with a membership category, we would likely resist changing the latter knowledge even if, empirically, we experience something that contradicts it. For example, if we associate the category elderly with decrement and illness, we may not modify it when we meet a healthy and active 80-year-old.

Differences are observable among membership categorization devices. In particular, some devices are reciprocally exclusive, whereas others show "gradeable qualities" (Coupland, Coupland, & Giles, 1991, p. 68). Membership categorization devices such as gender and race, for example, incorporate alternative categories like male–female and black–white, respectively. In contrast, membership categorization devices like age or social class do not provide clear cut, reciprocally exclusive alternatives; they are more blurred. That is, the categorization is relative to the subject who is producing it, as Sacks pointed out: "if you hear B categorize C as 'old,' then you would categorize B to decide how you would categorize C" (Sacks, 1992, Vol. 1, p. 45).

The process of identification is never clear-cut. For example, in their studies conducted with older people, the Couplands and their associates have noticed the "fluidity" of the process of identification in relation to membership categories use (Coupland, Coupland, Giles, & Henwood, 1991). The use of categories is far from being obvious and mechanical; instead, interpretative work is necessarily implied for the interlocutors; members can be seen performing "membership analysis upon each other" (Watson & Weinberg, 1982, p. 60).

The relevant problem, from theoretical and practical perspectives, is to understand the embeddedness of the use of membership categories in practical circumstances. As Sacks (1992) pointed out, "It is in principle never the case that persons are simply faced with applying a correct identification. And the procedures whereby they then go about selecting identifications in systematic ways, are a major problem for us" (Vol. 1, p. 588).

How do members go about selecting categories in relation to identity work, in the course of ordinary activities? Categories can be used through association or distancing, as well as through the interplay of both association and distancing. I am interested in the embeddedness of the use of categories in practical circumstances and, in particular, in relation to institutional influences on identity processes, because processes of social change and social reproduction become observable. It is to the treatment of this point that I now turn.

INSTITUTIONAL RELEVANCE
OF MEMBERSHIP CATEGORIES

According to ethnomethodology, the stable features of intitutional organizations are considered as an achievement of members, instead of a property of institutions. This implies a chronic problematicity in the management of everyday affairs that has to be concretely resolved by members with orientation to the features of the organization (Boden, 1994). They concretely orient their actions and discourses to what they perceive as the relevancies and scope of the organization.

Social interactions occasion the production of the social or institutional setting of action, as well as member's identities relevant to the occasion. In fact, it is only the analytical interest that can distinguish these aspects in what is a constant flow of action and discourses. My questions are: Do institutional subjects influence identity production processes? Do specific institutional discourses and practices contribute to shaping socially defined identities and if so, how? Moreover, does the negotiation of specific members' identities influence the production of actual, locally managed features of organizations and institutions?

I aim to answer these questions by exploring how institutional discourses and practices contribute to producing different older women's identities as a matter of ongoing negotiation, and how older women's perceived identities (life perspective, sphere of action, attitudes and skills) in turn contribute to shaping specific features of those same institutions.

Institutional settings, such as the Senior Citizen Centers and the Equal Opportunity Unit, are organized around identity-relevant membership categories. Discourses of "femininity" and "elderliness" shape these institutions and their aims; as such, these are two identity-relevant membership categories found in those institutions. Discourses and practices inherent to the aims and procedures of the institution should be relevant to membership categories, and thus relevant to identity construction. Discourses and

activities produced in those settings contribute to the social definition of
"elderliness" and "femininity." In fact, to define aims and objectives for an
Equal Opportunity Unit implies the production of discourses on the definition of "femininity." Determining the activities to be carried out in a Senior
Citizen Center itself contributes to the social definition of "elderliness."

Identities are ongoingly negotiated by members in and through social
interaction; moreover, we can see institutional subjects negotiating identities, for example, defining what "being old" or "being a woman" means.
Further, members' specific identities contribute to shaping features of those
same institutions. I aim to explore the reciprocal influence of subjects and
settings in producing each other interactionally in the course of conducting
ordinary activities.

In producing and reproducing the stable features of social reality, members are constantly engaged in a process of making sense, and making
decisions about personally meaningful courses of actions, in which feeling,
emotion, and personal values are implied. Identity production, probably
more than any other topic of study, allows the observation of intricate work
by members in reproducing the known features of social reality while
pursuing personal aims. For example, we can observe how members produce
what every-body-knows-about-elderly-persons while conducting everyday
activities, as well as how they dissociate from that social knowledge for
reasons bound to specific circumstances. Moreover, it is possible to look at
the reciprocal influence between members' identities and various institutions, such as the Equal Opportunity Unit and Senior Citizen Centers. In
short, studying identities allows researchers to observe the mechanisms of
social reproduction and maintenance, as well as the mechanisms that tend
to produce social change.

Through a detailed discourse analysis of transcripts from the videotapes,
this study will describe members' methods of negotiation of different identities, paying particular attention to institutional influence on that identity
work.

The second chapter, "Membership Categories in Identity Work," looks
at how age categories are used by older women in identity work and their
embeddedness in practical activities. Older women's association with the
detrimental aspects of the category are rare in the data I analyze, so two
instances in which the women attempt to deconstruct the negative aspects
of aging are particularly significant.

The next chapter, "When Is an Older Woman?," reports instances in
which association with this category is endorsed by the women when it
becomes institutionally relevant; moreover, I point out that if, on the one
hand, institutional intervention creates new activities and new opportunities of leadership for the women, then, on the other hand, institutional aims

and procedures impinge on women's priorities and understanding of issues at hand.

The relevance of gender in institutional conflicts is highlighted in the fourth chapter, "Institutional Conflicts and Gender Identification." This chapter shows how different institutional agencies fight over the space to be accorded to women for thier autonomous initiatives. I also point how institutional initiatives, the Action Project, affected women's perceived identities and modified their life perspectives.

The fifth chapter, "Members' Personal Identities and Institutions," is focused on the personal influence on institutional settings. If institutional influences contribute to shaping older women's identities, those same women in turn contribute to shaping specific features of these very institutions.

The Conclusion chapter underlines the practical usefulness of studying the processes of identity production for planning services and in the training of personnel working with the elderly.

2

Membership Categories in Identity Work

Sociolinguistic studies (Coupland & Coupland, 1990; Coupland, Coupland, & Giles, 1991; Taylor, 1992) have examined the conversational use of categories related to old age (which I conventionally refer to as the category *old*) in peer and intergenerational interaction in relation to identity-production processes. In particular, the Couplands and their associates have pointed out the variability in the use of the category and the different implications in identity work. Instances of either distancing from the category or denial of aging, as well as association with the detrimental characteristics of the category, are reported, with different implications for identity projections.

Association is predominant in Taylor's data, refering to mainly very old and frail elderly. Taylor has offered an insight into the level of suffering and despair that old age can represent for some people, as we can read in the following transcript:

> I'm so tired of these days that are so long, and there's no end to them, and they just go stretching on and on and on and on. I, I, I'm even worried now about next week. What am I gonna do next week? You know. Beside to go to the doctor, n'two doctors in one day. So it's all kinda crazy. But I do, I wish to die all the time. (Taylor, 1992, p. 506)

The data used in the aforementioned studies could be described as recordings of "personal encounters." The Couplands (1989, 1991a) and associates' studies were based on intergenerational first-acquaintance conversations, whereas Taylor (1992) used interview data of elderly, dependent homeowners and their student lodgers.

In the present study, the interactional encounters that were recorded refer to institutionally organized settings, that is, managing committee meetings and theater workshops. It is noticeable that in about 50 hours of recorded data for activities in which "elderliness" is central to the organizational feature of the setting (Committee meetings of the Older Women Group and of the Senior Citizen Centers) and to the definition of the task

14

at hand (Older Women's Action Project and the theater workshops), the terms *old, elderly, pensioner,* and the like, are seldom used. Moreover, in these data, alignment with the category "old," specifically with its negative attribution of decrement and ill health (Coupland, Coupland, & Giles, 1989), is absent, as are instances of self-handicapping (Coupland, Coupland, Giles, & Henwood, 1988) and self-stereotyping (Coupland, Coupland, Giles, & Henwood, 1988; Coupland, Coupland, Giles, Henwood, & Wiemann, 1988). The most common patterns of use of the category "old" observable in the data are distancing and denial of aging; association is limited to instances of use to justify limitations. However, association is also noticeable when the category "old" assumes an institutional relevance.

I would like to argue that these women, interviewed on a personal basis, might have offered accounts including a detrimental self-image. Different settings and activities may occasion contrasting self-images for the very same women. Therefore, I aim to highlight the occasioned nature of accounts; that is, that accounts are produced by members with reference to the specific eliciting situation, motives, and settings. It is difficult to imagine that painful self-disclosures such as those reported in Taylor's study could have occurred in the course of a committee meeting or during a theater workshop; they would have been incongruous given the occasion and the task at hand.

The occasioned nature of accounts does not pose only epistemological questions on how they can be analytically treated, but it also has very powerful practical implications. In this regard, issues related to establishing the veracity of accounts become close to irrelevant. As Silverman (1993) put it: "We need not hear interview responses simply as true or false reports on reality. Instead, we can treat such responses as *displays* of perspectives and moral forms" (p. 107). The matter is to understand the meaning and motivations of accounts in relation to the occasion, that is, what a person is doing with talk.

Practical implications within identity-relevant discourses are, then, powerful. For example, Coupland, Coupland, and Grainger (1991) found striking differences in the identity projection of an older woman in two different encounters: a stereotypic dependent image in the cross-generational conversation, and an active coping image in the peer–old encounter. Thus, some social enviroments and interactions foster positive self-image, whereas others do not; the consequences for one's life perspectives, such as integration or isolation, are predictable.

In analyzing the transcripts that follow, I wish to examine the embeddedness of the use of categories in practical activities. The use of categories is far from mechanical; rather, it is intertwined in a net of aims, motivations, moral relevances, and social and institutional practices. My interest is not as much in showing instances of variability in the use of categories, since such phenomena have already been documented extensively (Coupland,

Coupland, & Giles, 1991; Coupland, Coupland, & Grainger, 1991), but in looking at how this use of categories is embedded in members' practical activities and in specific institutional contexts.

It is during concrete, ordinary occasions that people either get trapped in stereotypic constructions that limit and restrict themselves, or are able to skillfully play with categories, producing a "space" for positive self-images, announcing new and exciting life perspectives. Such constructions are not produced "in people's heads"; rather, they are bound to specific social and institutional settings as well to concrete circumstances as the product of members' interpretative work in relation to specific activities.

It is through the variability of the use of categories that either marginalization and exclusion of older people, or, instead, integration and social resourcefulness, are conversationally produced.

In this chapter I look at how distancing and association with the membership category "old" are managed by members in relation to identity work, highlighting in particular its embeddedness in practical activities. Instances of association with the category, when it becomes institutionally significant, are examined in detail in chapter 3.

JUSTIFYING LIMITATIONS

Disclosure of chronological age is reported to be often used to account for ill health (Coupland, Coupland, & Giles, 1989). Old age and consequent frailty and decline are also used by caregivers to account for "questionable behavior" of older people (Taylor, 1992). In this study, the membership category "old" is rarely used by the women to refer to themselves. When used, it is generally implied rather than expressed explicitly; in some instances, reference to old age is used to justify the women's perceived limitations.

The following passage is a long and complex transcript, where age and social class identities are projected in the context of a very animated discussion. The women are evaluating the latest public performance of their singing groups. Lidia has reported negative comments from the public and now is envisaging future prospects for the singing group (transcript notations are reported in Appendix A):

> **Lidia:**   we could turn, towards for example choir, not a real choir, no pop
>   song, so just to sing, and who sings must be able to sing,
> **Researcher:** well no
> **Lidia:**   you need [(   )
> **Ilda:**   [you cannot demand this

Alma:	[madam ((raising her hand)) this this this I take the floor I am sorry, consider madam once I told a lawyer, madam I don't understand you, that I don't understand you, it could happen, right but that you don't understand me you are a great ignorant, excuse me, here we are all,
Ilda:	elderly
Alma:	no one is a singer ((Ilda nods)) and who does not understand us ((sign with her hand meaning "to go away"))
Lidia:	I didn't make myself understood
Alma:	((Alma turns)) ( ) eh [because you cannot throw away a word ((sign with her hand that means "throw away"))
Lidia:	[I don't mean that you don't understand me, [I didn't make myself understood
Ilda:	[( ) it's not possible
Lidia:	madam not everyone can write poetry
Alma:	umh ((Alma nods))
Lidia:	[is that right?
Ilda:	[OK [no that's right
Lidia:	[therefore you cannot pretend that a person that cannot write poetry ((Alma nods)) will start writing poetry
Alma:	umh
Lidia:	voice, is a gift just like that of writing poetry who hasn't got it cannot invent it then since it is not compulsory to sing the singing group should [be made of persons ( )
Alma:	[I don't no no no I don't agree [I don't no no no I don't agree then we bury the group here I am sorry
Ilda:	[no no no

There are some comments exchanged on the necessity of joint rehearsal for all the groups before performances, then Alma continues to express her disagreement with Lidia's proposal:

Alma:	it's the only thing that would keep me away ever if you say to do discriminations, no way we are all a group, for the good and bad fortune and all a group we have to remain
Officer:	ss sss ( ) just a moment just a moment
Clelia:	there is another thing, that whoever didn't like it. Can shut up that I mean we are not young any more [( ) ((everybody talking))
Ida:	[the voice collapses, as everything else
Clelia:	am I right? and everyone tries to do her best

Ida: certainly

Alma: I cannot sing, I only went up to grade four, I cannot write poetry
         (   ) [are you joking
Clelia: [(   ) for older people, we should consider that
         (12/18/92 Committee meeting of the Action Project)

Lidia proposes a new composition of the singing group based on ability, *who sings must be able to sing; The researcher*[1] *signals disagreement, well no.* Other negative comments follow, *you cannot demand this*; in particular Alma comes out with a passionate protest, *((raising her hand)) this this this I take the floor.* Not only the contents, but the style, the argumentative structure, the use of gestures, and the use of regional dialect (unfortunately impossible to render in the English translation) all contribute to producing different social class identities for Lidia and Alma.

Alma starts her speech reporting an episode of misunderstanding between herself and a lawyer. The sentence, *that you don't understand me you are a great ignorant,* is constructed against the background of common knowledge of a lawyer as supposedly a highly educated person. Alma argues that the lawyer was not justified in showing inability in understanding a less educated person (herself). However, the reverse would have been admissible, *that I don't understand you, it could happen.* In this way Alma projects her own identity as less educated, a significant attribution for "social class" identification. Her next argumentative move is to include "being able to sing" in "being educated," consequently implying that more musically educated people should be able to understand less musically educated people. In the instant of hesitation, *here we are all,* Ilda completes the sentence with, *elderly,* introducing for the first time the use of the category "old," apparently to justify the unsuccessful performance. Finishing each others' sentences is a practice widely used by the women, as will be obvious in the course of the analysis. In this case Alma sticks with her argument, *no one is a singer,* and is sustained by Ilda, *((Ilda nods)),* and finishes establishing the exclusion of those who will not accept a comprehensive membership policy by which people may participate independent of their singing skills, *and who do not understand us ((sign with her hand meaning "to go away")).* Notice that logical connections are never made explicit: Sentences are juxtaposed in a strictly consequent sequence though, and gesture is used as a structural component of the sentence, not simply as an emphatic device.

---

[1]Notice, that I am not using the first person, although "researcher" clearly refers to me, because I don't want to advocate any superior understanding of the text, but only what is available to observation through the development of the turns at talk (see Bilmes, 1992; Schegloff, 1988). I am one participant among the others.

The distinction proposed by Lidia, *I don't mean that you don't understand me, I didn't make myself understood*, seems to endorse Alma's argument that more educated people have to make a special effort in explaining themselves to less educated people, signaling consequently her higher level of education. Moreover, in Lidia's argumentation all logical connections among sentences are made explicit, and no gesture substitutes for talk. It is particularly in contrast to Alma's expressive strategies that Lidia appears "more educated," with clear implications for class identification.

Ambiguity is produced through the use of the term *pretend*, in relation to writing poetry and singing, a term that can mean either to allege falsely or to demand, *you cannot pretend that a person that cannot write poetry . . . will start writing poetry*. The real argument proposed by Lidia is excellence of the product; she appears to be saying, *"If we want a good performance, we need good singers,"* but that is not stated openly. Instead, she says that singing, like writing poetry, is a gift; consequently, nobody is obliged/has to pretend to be able to write or sing (*cannot invent it/it is not compulsory to sing*). But just as a person who is not skilled in writing poetry can still want to do it, so it is for singing. Excellence of the product remains a hidden agenda.

Alma continues expressing her strong disagreement, *I don't no no no I don't agree*, and she threatens to dissolve the partnership, *we bury the group here*. Then, after a brief discussion on the importance of rehearsals, she continues her argument, using Biblical overtones. She threatens again to leave the group, *it's the only thing that would keep me away*, if discriminatory criteria are established for the composition of the singing groups. She underlines the moral character of the enterprise, *we are all a group, for the good and bad fortune and all a group we have to remain*.

To support Alma's argument against discrimination, Clelia joins in, using reference to old age to justify limitations in the performance. It is necessary to point out that Clelia is among the youngest in the group, being in her 50s. It recurs throughout the data that reference to the category "old" is more frequently used by younger group members. Indirect reference to "old age," *we are not young any more*, is used to account for the inadequacy of the performance of their singing groups. Ida reinforces Clelia's statement by mentioning various negative aspects of elderliness: *The voice collapses, as everything else*. The image of collapsing can be associated with bodily appearance; this is particularly salient to women's picturing of old age (Kamler & Feldman, 1995).

Alma continues with her protest, this time explicitly stating her limited education, *I was in the fourth class of primary school*; she rebels, *are you joking*, to the implications of Lidia's argument, *I cannot sing, I cannot write poetry*. In fact, Alma also likes to write poetry. In the next turn by Clelia, old age is again mentioned as a sufficient justification for special consideration, *for older people, we should consider that*.

In this transcript we have seen how age and class identity are constructed in and through the argumentative features of the exchange. Limitations due to old age are used as an argument to sustain an inclusive policy in group composition; moreover, lack of education, a social class identifier, is applied for the same purposes. Identity work is achieved in relation to the occasion, the committee's evaluation of the singing performance. The outcome of the discussion has possible concrete implications for the women's lives: exclusion or inclusion in the singing group. Age and social class identities are produced in the process of dealing with practical ordinary events as serious matters that have concrete consequences for the participants.

In this transcript, the use of categories and identity projections is strictly connected to the activity that is being carried out in the specific occasion: "arguing." From this perspective, the detrimental attributions that come with the category "old" are in some way bracketed, in the sense that they can be mainly interpreted as moves in a specific argumentative strategy. Consequently, it is understandable that, on other occasions, these very same women forcefully refuse to use the category "old" to refer to themselves, or they attribute negative aspects of old age to "out-group" members but not themselves, as are described later (Coupland, Coupland, Giles, & Henwood, 1991).

DISTANCING

Instances of use of the category "old" to designate "the others" (the very old) are reported in the literature: "Very often 'old' is invoked as an outgroup category, even by speakers we are referring to as elderly" (Coupland, Coupland, & Giles, 1991, p. 60). Distancing is achieved by association of the category "old" with its negative stereotypical attributions (frailty, dependence, ill health, loneliness), but designating other members with it. By not advocating co-membership in this category, such speakers project a positive personal identity for themselves.

The gradable properties of age categories (Coupland, Coupland, & Giles, 1991) are particularly evident when out-group members can be designated with the same membership category. A decremental perspective is evoked with the out-group member occupying the very end of the scale, but decline remains impending for any member, as can be seen in the next transcript.

In the last meetings in 1993, before the summer break, the discussion developed around the following year's program. Rita mentioned activities aimed at bringing solidarity among generations. Here, she is explaining why she thinks they are relevant:

Rita: I'd like from the young people a bit more sympathy for the elderly
( ) we can still defend ourselves
Officer: [please, please ((the talking stops))
Rita: [but the elderly who stay inside the house and do not go out any
more, and they marginalize themselves because, there is no
communication we as much as we can do the children one, either
because you are busy or because you are in a hurry or you have
to run here and well sometimes the elderly stay alone for hours,
inside the house, the memory fades more and more, who can offer
a bit of of, of comfort perhaps make them speak about the old
days, eh only the young people
(5/10/93 Committee meeting of the Action Project)

The word "elderly" is followed by a distancing move, *we can still defend ourselves,* that projects a differentiation among two different groups of older people. Consequently, the negative attribution of marginalization (*do not go out any more, no communication*), loneliness (*the elderly stay alone for hours*), and forgetfulness (*the memory fades*) do not refer to the in-group, but to the "others," the very old. Nevertheless, consider that *we can still defend ourselves* conveys a temporary status that projects similar negative perspectives onto Rita's future life (Taylor, 1992). Thus, the passage through "natural lifetime" (Baker, 1984) is used as a resource in the talk, projecting decrement as a natural development (Coupland & Coupland, 1989). Moreover, different degrees of busyness are distributed to the different "stages of life," *either because you are busy or because you are in a hurry or you have to run.* This account can therefore be heard as a moral tale (Baker & Keogh, 1995; Silverman, 1987, 1993) in which different moral duties are allocated and suspended. In particular, the care and support of the very old, a woman's duty (Facchini & Scortegagna, 1993; Laws, 1995; Mengani & Lamura, 1995) is alleviated from the busy adult, and the responsibility for communicating with the elderly is passed on to the supposedly disengaged young.

Similar attributions of sadness and solitude are projected onto institutionalized elderly, depicted in the next passages. The group is discussing activities of solidarity among generations to be carried out in relation to the Action Project:

Tina: I'd also like to go to this little old people [( ) I'd like it
(Delia): [eeh I have
Alba: did you read it Irma, [Irma
Tina: [because we also need to think about them,
Diana: this with the elderly (I say) something we did it more than with
the children=

Officer:	=eh yes
Tina:	but not I was saying
Diana:	we too we too
(Ida):	our Center too
Woman:	[poor elderly
Officer:	[( ) at San Marco they said [(that they did it)
Researcher:	[but this is an excellent idea [because if there isn't
Ida:	[of course of course
Researcher:	soli solidarity among older people
Ida:	yes yes
Tina:	I'd like [(very much)
Woman:	[( )
Tina:	to do something because they go there, they do some, [something for example
Researcher:	[that's great
Tina:	[I saw a sketch (there was)
Nina:	[I also went (to) to to perform (to the older people). [Aaat, aat, at Fonte Novo
Tina:	[there was one already (usually) for Christmas all these sketches are performed and we could also do go to once [to these
Ida:	[to bring a bit of,
Tina:	of cheerfulness
Ida:	of consolation
Tina:	to bring something and to bring a bit of cheerfulness to this little old people don't we
Researcher:	of course ((whispering general comments))
Tina:	I'd like I'd ( )
Officer:	well oh, there is this to say too, that it is true that the solidarity among generations,
	...
Officer:	then, solidarity among generations it is true does not mean only [(between older people)
Woman:	[with young people ( ) ((whispering))
Officer:	because moreover the (fourth) age is not who knows which hence it can also be solidarity with the more [old
Nina:	[with the more old

(10/9/92 Committee meeting of the Action Project)

Tina expresses the desire *to go to this little old people*. The expression "little old people" blurs the distinction between a patronizing tone and caring content. This ambiguity has been noticed in studies of baby talk to the elderly (Caporael, 1981; Caporael & Culbertson, 1983; Cohen & Faulkner, 1986; Hepworth, 1996). For example, Caporael and Culbertson (1986) noticed that, although baby talk can be heard containing a "depreciatory message . . . the register is primarily associated with nurturant affect" (p. 100). Considering the likely good intention of the speaker, talking of *little old people* may nevertheless predict and produce dependency.

The whole discourse in the preceding passage is strongly inscribed in a moral universe. Tina presents visiting the elderly as a moral duty, *we also need to think about them*, and in doing so she is actually constructing "them" as an out-group. Some lines later, this sense of compassion and moral obligation is increased by a woman saying, *poor elderly*. Many interjections state how Senior Citizen Centers have participated in activities involving the elderly, *this with the elderly (I say) something we did it more than with the children; our Center too*. The researcher's turn introduces a different perspective, by talking about *solidarity among older people*; in fact, she includes present group members as well as the "others" in the one category. This is not picked up, except by the officer, another younger group member, at the end of the passage.

Tina goes on to describe a possible activity, a theater performance, to be carried out for the benefit of the older people. By saying, *I also went . . . to perform . . . at Fonte Novo*, Nina makes explicit, for the first time in this sequence, who the "elderly" being discussed are: They are institutionalized elderly (Fonte Nuovo is a geriatric home in Perugia).

The reference to Christmas serves to inscribe the issue of "visiting the elderly" in a moral and religious context: doing-good-deeds-for-Christmas, *for Christmas all these sketches are performed and we could also do go. . . .* In this passage, in which Ida and Tina finish each other's sentences, *to bring a bit of . . . cheerfulness . . . of consolation*, "the elderly" are constructed as in need of being cheered up and comforted, thus implying their sadness and suffering. In particular, the expression, *to bring a bit of . . . consolation* may remind participants of the Christian precept of "comfort the suffering." I believe that this discourse of providing assistance would be a lot less salient if the speakers had been men, who are not generally perceived as caregivers.

In the end, the officer expresses the policy of the group in relation to solidarity among generations by naming "the others" as *the more old*. The formulation is supported by Nina. It is important to point out that chronological age is not the main issue here in determining the difference between older people and "the more old." Although in the group there are many women in their 50s and 60s, there are also many in their 70s and some 80 years old. It is the "institutionalized elderly" who are being treated as a homogenuous group with typical—that is, stereotyped—needs.

This stereotypical view of the "very old" or "institutionalized old people," who are constructed as an out-group, has double implications for identitification work. On the one hand, distancing themselves from the category allows the women to project positive self-images of effective adults. On the other hand, decrement is still impending and, as in the first transcript analyzed, it is managed as a threat to a positive self-projection, *we can still defend ourselves*. Thus, it appears that stereotyping and, consequently, marginalization of older people is not only an issue at an intergenerational level, but it can occur among older people themselves (Levin & Levin, 1980).

The accounts analyzed here are constructed against the background of a moral order; they are primarily moral accounts (Silverman, 1993) in which the "sad," "suffering," and "lonely" elderly must be assisted. It is a moral order that is more relevant to women than to men; in fact, the care of the elderly is considered a woman's duty (Paoletti, 1997b). This has a correspondence in actual gender composition in the profession of caregivers: By and large, formal and informal care of the elderly is carried out by women.

Distancing from the category "old" allows members to project a positive self-image, attributing negative characteristics of the category to out-group members. "Denial of aging," as we will see in the following section, has similar effects on identity projection; that is, it presents a positive self-image, while postponing decline.

DENIAL OF AGING

The explicit rejection of membership in the category "old," is a widely documented phenomenon in the literature (Bultena & Powers, 1978; Coupland, Coupland, & Giles, 1991; Kamler, 1995). Old age is often seen as a natural decremental process, an ineluctable decline in health and competence (Bultena & Powers, 1978; Coupland & Coupland, 1990). Gerontological studies contribute to this view of aging as a deviant phenomenon (Green, 1993) by characterizing it primarily in terms of senescence and ill health.

In Bultena and Powers' 10-year longitudinal study, intended to measure age identity through self-categorizations, age categories are considered discrete, well-defined cataloguers. However, when I use the term *denial of aging* as a descriptor of various members' activities, I refer to a substantially different conception of age categories as blurred, fuzzy-edged, and interactionally defined. Such categories constitute background knowledge, and their specific management in conversation allows members to negotiate personal identities in and through the unfolding of particular conversations (Schenkein, 1978).

There are some examples in the data where the category "old" is explicitly rejected by the women as a term properly referring to themselves. A particularly relevant instance is offered in a discussion of the choice of the name of the women's group in Perugia that had to be officially constituted. Names that would include the word *old* were only proposed by younger group members; these were decisively rejected by the older women. The discussion lasted for about 15 minutes. The following transcript is the most significant part of that interactional sequence:

Social worker:	international Italian solidarity association or group women or older women right?
Woman:	yes women
Women:	women
Teacher:	women
Social worker:	older women is not that great
Women:	no no [no ((aloud speaking all together))
Woman:	[are you joking!
Alba:	[(they are not old at all) her her her they are all young
Officer:	older women
Sonia:	eh that's right ((smiling))
Alba:	the ladies, [are all young
Pietro:	[where are the old people ((smiling))
Officer:	over 50 years [(they are not a lot)
Pietro:	[eeh! ( ) ((gesture to indicate exaggeration))
Elia:	(my husband's grandmother) would say what old, old is the shell (2/5/94 Committee meeting of the Action Project)

Women is explicitly stated as the preferred word for the participants to refer to themselves. When the social worker proposes "older women" as a dispreferred term, *older women is not that great*, she is strongly supported, *no no no ((aloud speaking all together)); are you joking.*

A quite intricate series of turns at talk follows. Alba's remark, *(they are not old at all) her her her they are all young*, lists the women considered young in the group, but she excludes herself. This is a move in a "*ritualistic* sequence" (Coupland, Coupland, Giles, & Henwood, 1991) to elicit protest and therefore her inclusion, as can be seen from the following turns at talk. Sonia comments on Alba's remark, *eh that's right ((smiling))*, provide an ironical inflection to the coversation; she can be seen doing "pretending" (Baker, 1984), that is, signaling pretended membership in the "young" category with respect to lifetime positioning, and in this way actually distancing herself from it. This is not what Alba was expecting; therefore, she produces the next significant move, restating *the ladies, are all young*, apparently including herself this time. As others have noted, being considered young is salient for women, particularly in relation to the importance bestowed on bodily appearance (Kamler & Feldman, 1995).

Meanwhile, the officer proposes the use of the term *older women*, but she is not supported. This is noticeable, because she generally has a large following in the committee. Pietro replies ironically to the officer, *where are the old people ((smiling))*. The gradable qualities of the category "old" (Coupland, Coupland, Giles, & Henwood, 1991) are made explicit in the next turns at talk: The officer defines elderliness as starting after 50 years of age, *over 50 years*, but Pietro does not agree, *eeh! ( ) ((gesture to indicate exaggeration))*. To determine when old age does start is a problem for all practical purposes, whether at a personal, social, or institutional level.

Finally, Elia cites the saying, *what old, old is the shell*, which at the same time negates and affirms membership in the category "old." In Italian there are several expressions similar to "old is the shell," for example, "old are the clothes." They all refer to the distinction between appearing old physically and being young in energy and spirit.

This duplicity in association and rejection of the category resulted very clearly in the name that was finally chosen for the older women's group in Perugia: Associazione Italiana Donne Attive/Anziane (AIDA); in English it reads: Italian Association of Active/Older Women. The final "A" of the association name carries this duplicity. The decision to include the word *older*, despite the aversion expressed by the women, was due to institutional reasons, such as prospective links to European elderly networks, access to special funding, and the like. The word *active* allows the camouflage; in fact, the word could be omitted, insofar as a second "A" has not been added to the acronym.

The distancing mentioned previously moves from the category "old," as well as the denial of aging, have been shown to be used conversationally by members to project images of themselves as effective adults, proposing positive self-identifications. A similar combination of association and dissociation from elderliness is achieved in the talk reported in the next transcript. In this case, a criticism of the negative characterization of the category is attempted.

DECONSTRUCTING AGING

The women were planning a TV program for a local station in which they were invited to take part; in this excerpt, Rita strongly supports the idea of including the topic of solidarity among generations:

> **Rita:** I felt my only satisfaction, these days going to visit schools with these youngsters
> **Alba:** that's true that's true
>   ((all talking at once commenting))

Lola: [( )
Rita: [( ) with these generations with these discourses of the young-
sters with the elderly [to limit a bit this elderliness to take out a
bit
Emma: [(to overcome the generational)
Rita: the old from the word because, because we are, we are old well
but with a lot of experience that we, one could, one could give a
lot yet you know, a lot of teaching
(10/5/93 Committee meeting of the Action Project)

Rita starts with a mild dissociation from the category, *to limit a bit this elderliness*; then she specifies: *to take out a bit the old from the word.* This very vividly expresses the dissociation from the detrimental attribution of the category "old," as the word *negative* could subsitute for it. She seems to be proposing to take out the negative aspect from the word *elderliness*. She accepts membership in the category, *we are old*, but wants to dissociate herself from the detrimental characterization of the term and to highlight, instead, its positive aspects. In fact, the explicit association with the category is immediately followed by its commonsense positive characterization, *with a lot of experience*. Denial of aging is not the only means of projecting a positive social image: Subversion of the category has been attempted as well.

Positive characterizations of the category "old" are quite rare. The next transcript can certainly be considered one such exception.

Generally positive self-appraisals as an older person are constructed though comparisons with negative stereotypic constructions of old age (Bultena & Powers, 1978; Coupland, Coupland, & Giles, 1991). In the following case, a more positive life situation is directly experienced by the subject: Relationally, economically, and socially, life is said to improve with increased age. Recall that similar accounts were reported in the prologue, taken from the interviews carried out in the pilot study. I conclude this chapter with this rather funny and provocative transcript, the only one in the data in which association with elderliness is invoked. It sounds like a manifesto:

Lola: listen, I the people of my age ( ) now the, we older people have
come out of our shells and we are beautiful strong and spunky
and not any more with lice on our heads but well groomed by the
hairdresser,
Emma: I said it also [in my programme
Lola: [we have started to experience this after we were
60 years old, and we are ready to help the young people boys
(girls) everybody who needs it
(10/5/93 Committee meeting of the Action Project)

Lola is in her 70s and she feels she is, together with other older people, *beautiful strong and spunky.* She describes these positive connotations as the outcome of a process, *we older people have come out of our shells.* The whole passage gives a sense of progression from a negative to a positive condition, in particular, *not any more with lice on our heads but well groomed by the hairdresser,* hinting at improved economic as well as social situations. The present positive condition is explicitly associated with elderliness, *we have started to experience this after we were 60 years old.*

This passage projects a very different life perspective from Rita's, in which marginalization, loneliness, and fading memory were ahead for her. Here, solidarity with young people is the prospect. In order to help them reach the positive situation she has obtained after many struggles during the course of her life, Lola asserts *we are ready to help the young people.* In this way, Lola also gives a nontraditional twist to the womanly caring role for the young, that is, a "political" intergenerational solidarity.

Risks in celebrating old age and in constructing it positively, have been pointed out (Baltes & Carstensen, 1996; Coupland & Coupland, 1994; Kamler & Feldman, 1995), but I don't believe that they are greater than those implied in negative constructions of elderliness, with their danger of a self-fulfilling prophecy (Levin & Levin, 1980). Above all, it is important to highlight the degree of variability in older people's conditions. Older people are not a homogenous group; studies have shown that chronological age (Bengtson, 1973; Montepare & Lachman, 1989; Rubin & Rubin, 1986) is not always a significant indicator of elderly condition. Moreover, gender differences have been grossly overlooked, as pointed out earlier. There is clearly a range of possibilities connected to being old: differences in life perspectives, available opportunities, and activities.

From the analysis of the preceding transcripts, we gain an idea of the degree of variability in the use of the category "old." It has been shown how the use of the category is specifically related to the occasion, the setting of the encounter, and the conversational purposes of the interlocutors. Use of categories is not clear-cut, nor mechanical, but achieved through interpretative work by members in producing as well as understanding talk. In fact, categories could be considered as a background knowledge by which actual states of affairs and identities are managed on the ground through moment-to-moment interactional production (Schenkein, 1978).

The stable character of membership categories is in contrast with the variability of their conversational use. That is, their commonsense meaning stands in opposition to their malleability in allowing members to produce highly individualized and differentiated identities. Both the possibility of mere reproduction of typified and stereotypic categorization, as well as distancing and differentiation from them, are conversationally available.

Furthermore, the use of categories and, therefore, identification processes, is inscribed in a moral universe. Moral duties are attached to specific identities; to endorse an identity equally implies the attribution of certain moral duties to the subject. Such tasks are gender specific; for example, caring duties are generally attributed to women (Paoletti, 1997b).

The analysis has shown how the women project positive personal identities, differentiating themselves from old age categories and from related category-bound activities. The images of older women emerging from the transcripts analyzed are ones of busy and effective adults. Images of dependency, sickness, and loneliness are not part of the picture. On the other hand, these women construct stereotyped identities for the "other," the very old or institutionalized elderly.

It is in this double-faced character of categorization processes that complex interactional phenomena at a group level, such as marginalization or racism, can be understood. It is the association with stereotyped meanings of the category that produce de-individualization and therefore exclusion.

Despite the overall trend of dissociation from the category that has been illustrated herein, there are occasions in which "being an older woman" is endorsed and becomes significant. The next chapter examines how the category "old" is used when it becomes an institutionally relevant category.

3

When Is an Older Woman?

In the preceding chapter I examined some features of the use of the category "old" in relation to identity processes. Because of the category's negative connotations, positive self-image and age identity as an effective adult were shown to be achieved by distancing and dissociation from it. In particular I have shown how the term "old" is despised more or less openly by the women and rejected as a category referring to themselves. However, that data also indicate that the category becomes relevant, meaningful—even, in some way, desired and sought after—when it becomes institutionally relevant. This chapter examines how age categories are treated differently by the women when they are institutionally relevant. Some instances in which an institutional definition of older women is conversationally produced in the course of the ordinary conduct of the Action Project committee meetings are analyzed. On the one hand, insitutional intervention can positively mobilize women's perceived identities, opening new opportunities for action for them. On the other hand, institutional terms of relevancies can prevail negatively on older women's understanding of the issues in relation to a particular interaction. Institutional influences on identity production appear to be complex and multifaceted.

WHEN BEING OLD MATTERS

In the analysis of the transcripts that follows, I point out how "elderliness" can assume a character of "prestige" when it gives access to special institutionally designed activities, or to particular benefits or services. In these instances, it is endorsed by the women with no hesitation.

In the course of the Action Project there were numerous occasions in which interest was expressed by various institutions about the Older Women's Group in Perugia: The group was invited to international conferences; magazines for elderly people called the women for interviews; local radio shows and TV programs sought their contributions; their singing and theater groups were invited to perform in geriatric homes, schools, and senior citizen centers; and nursing schools sought contact. Through the

Action Project, "being an older woman" became an object of interest for a variety of institutions. This interest contributed to defining what "being an older woman" meant and could mean, and projected new, different, and appealing life perspectives for the women involved.

Requests for contributions by the Older Women's Action Project to various local, national, or international events were routinely presented and discussed in the committee meetings. The following transcripts offer two examples. In the first, the officer is soliciting the women's participation in an international initiative of the EC:

> **Officer:** within the initiatives for the European Year of the Elderly, a train is organized that will leave from Paris and will reach I don't know how many European countries how many countries will it reach Mira?
>
> **Mira:** sixteen
>
> **Officer:** sixteen European nations, eee, among which Milan I mean Italy through Milan it will be in Milan the eighth of October. We sent a bit of our things because we thought to interpret the will of all of you that the European Action Project was represented in this train
>
> **Nina:** yes
>
> **Officer:** isn't it? oh, uum we made the impossible there too because they wanted it so but not really so, not too much but not too little, eee and well we tried to please them this morning in their last phone call they said that they will show a poster, with some photos of the main stages of the Project and also the material that I sent them that is the booklet the booklet with the contact with the other Nations the booklet of Perugia of course the research of Isabella Paoletti all that (which   ), they will show all that we sent them. It wouldn't be a bad idea that on the eighth of October [someone went to Milan
>
> **Ida:**   [(someone   )
>
> **Women:**   [(   )
>
> **Officer:** well for for the Office Mira will go. That's it that's it, think about it
>
> (9/15/93 Committee meeting of the Action Project)

The use of the category "elderly," in designating an international event, *the European Year of the Elderly,* here loses all of its negative connotations. In fact, the women are asked to take part (*It wouldn't be a bad idea that . . . someone went to Milan*) in a prestigious initiative (*a train is organized that will leave from Paris and will reach . . . sixteen European nations*) that will draw attention to their work. This request implies traveling and being a spokesperson, both activities that are quite unusual for most of the women in the group. Membership in the category here allows access to a desirable activity, and a very unconventional image of older women is projected.

Notice the institutional use of the pro-term *we* (Sacks, 1992; Watson, 1987) in the sentence *we sent a bit of our things because we thought to interpret the will of all of you that the European Action Project was represented in this train*. It is used to designate the Equal Opportunity Unit, *we sent, we thought*, but it is made ambiguous by the possessive *our things*, in which the reference is clearly shifted to the Action Project women's group. In fact, *our things* is further made explicit by listing the objects that were sent, mainly women's works for the Action Project. (The issue of the institutional ownership of women's work is developed in the last section of this chapter.)

International events such as this particular one, or such as participation in conferences and exchange visits among groups of older women in various European countries, were seen as desired and prestigious events by the women. At the same time, many local initiatives were also appreciated. These too were designed to bring out women's experience and their contributions, as appears clear from the next transcript.

The women associated with the Action Project were asked to intervene in a training course for nurses and various other personnel working with elderly people, to offer their perspective on the condition of elderly people. In the following excerpt, they are discussing how to participate. The officer suggests a slide show, the result of a photographic workshop in which the women were invited to reminisce about some old photos of theirs:

Officer:	it's, a, a program of stories of memories knowledge through memories from eeem, us to the young the young, in this case are, above all, persons who will then work with older people, eh therefore [from nurses
Woman:	[they are students
Office:	to social worker,
Woman:	students
Officer:	or students of of of of various disciplines who then either from a cultural or physical caring point of view might work with older people in short the intention is to make aware these persons that's of the, true, reality I mean the true meaning [( ) the older person therefore is not only a ( )
Women:	[( )

(10/12/93 Committee meeting of the Action Project)

The hesitation, *eeem, us*, in pronouncing the pro-term can be interpreted as signaling a disturbance in the categorization process. The category "old" is clearly implied in the use of the pro-term, because of the presence of the contrasting category, "young," both of which are drawn from the same "stage of life" membership categorization device (Sacks, 1972). It is also part of the category-bound activity (Sacks, 1972) "passing on memories." Boden and Bielby (1983, 1986) have pointed out the relevance of the past as a topic and a resource in elderly talk. Therefore, the officer might have hesitated in including herself in the category, being a younger group member.

No association is made between present group members and *older people,*" who are constructed as beneficiaries of the review services and assistance offered by the students and professionals who will be in the audience for the slide presentation. Instead, expressing the aim of the event, *the intention is to make aware these persons that's of the, true, reality I mean the true meaning . . . older person,* the women's potential contribution is broached and they are constructed as the repository of the "true" knowledge about older people's conditions. Two different groups of elderly people are thus projected: in-group and knowledgeable elderly, and out-group sick and dependent elderly (Coupland, Coupland, & Giles, 1991). No explicit use of old age categories is made in the transcript to designate the in-group, which allows the participants to conversationally produce the distinction between in-group and out-group while avoiding negative associations for the in-group.

In both of the preceding passages, institutional interests mobilize the older women's projected identities: New and interesting activities become accessible, and their contribution is sought out. To be part of the group, to carry out those activities, is rewarding and desirable. Association with old age categories loses its negative connotations or, more explicitly, those connotations are skillfully suspended, and old age assumes a character of prestige.

In other instances, association with the category "old" is seen positively because of more general institutional dynamics. Older people as a group are the benificiaries of government services and specific legislation. They are the object of interest of several different institutions, in various ways. For example, older people represent a conspicuous part of the electorate, and for this reason they are of interest to political institutions. In the course of the last meeting, Enza reports news of a political action from a local Member of Parliament:

> ((all the women are talking together))
> Enza: ((talking softly to the officer)) Rossi told me that, the Government the Italian Parliament (the new Italian Parliament) is creating a commission
> Officer: excuse me she is saying an important thing
> Enza: very important that, the Member of Parliament Rossi, told me that the Parliament the new Governament is looking into the

Nina:
Enza:

possibility of letting us have back the international card for elderly people for us elderly people a card, um an international card that we can travel in various countries=

=with special discounts for elderly people good

((nodding)) it's doing, everything to let us have it back (this card) (5/2/94 Committee meeting of the Action Project)

Notice that Enza not only describes what she says is important news, but she also constructs it as such. She reinforces the officer's statement, *she is saying an important thing,* with, *very important* and she changes from an informal whisper to the officer, *Rossi told me,* to a public announcement to the group, *the Member of Parliament Rossi, told me.*

"Older people" is constructed here as a homogeneous group, a recipient of favors, *letting us have back the international card for elderly people,* that other persons with specific institutional roles are able to obtain through effort, *it's doing, everything to let us have back (this card).* Membership in the category is not questioned, but is rather underlined, *the international card for elderly people for us elderly people a card.* The pro-term *us* makes explicit membership in the category "old"; Enza is thus clearly "doing inclusion" (Watson, 1987). Further, Nina comments positively on the prospect, *special discounts for elderly people good.*

Traveling is made relevant to "older people" by this discussion; the elderly are treated as an homogeneous group, and they are constructed both as recipients of favors and as actively engaged in life.

Could the above passage be heard as a piece of electioneering propaganda for *the Member of Parliament Rossi?* There is no evidence that the audience heard it this way, and in no way am I attributing such an intention to the speaker. By asking such a question, however, I wish to draw attention to the possibility that if older people can find "elderliness" appealing in relation to the grant of special benefits by some institutions, they then become of interest to these institutions in various ways. In the next passage, older people are constructed as both the beneficiaries of medical services and as a potential market for a private medical enterprise.

The following transcript is taken from a managing committee's meeting of the Senior Citizen Center of Ponte Felcino (in the transcript, C is a male committee member). Lidia is informing the group about her recent encounter with a physician:

Lidia:

so this doctor introduced himself, precisely because he was contacted for this reason and then I thought that once we could just like that afternoon that was so interesting with Doctor

Giuliano Dini and the other dietician he could also tell us about sickness concerning to tooo our age, the romantic pains as we call them

Rita: [(not very) romantic they are (unfortunately)

Lidia: [and this doctor guess that I did not know anything about and in fact I immediately engaged him to do it myself without going to the various chiropractic Centers this one is in Ponte Felcino, he does magnetotherapy does iontophoresis he comes at home and he does it also at his place the whole thing for ten thousand liras one hour of magnetotherapy for ten thousand liras I was amazed and then I got informed and they told me that he is an extremely good and professional person ((all talking at once))

Lidia: ((talking over the general whispering)) so since to go to the clinic at the Orthopedic Center, you need to get angry to have this possibility, who is not exempted pays the "ticket" because you pay it, eh, I repeat it you have to take a bus or two to get to Umbrian Orthopedic Center that is in Solatia Street down there near the veterinarian clinic [you know, it is very complicated

Rita: [excuse me mrs. Lidia one thousand [for what?

C member: [for a treatment

Rita: [for the massage

Lidia: [ten thousand liras for an hour of magnetotherapy thing that at [USSL you get 15 treatments

Rita: [yes, I know for that I already have the appointment

C member: [for a treatment

Rita: but what about massage?

Lidia: he does physiotherapy iontophoresis massage therapy therefore also manipulations, then I repeat it, if we ask him to come one day he will explain it to us.

(4/19/93 Managing committee meeting of the Senior Center of Ponte Felcino)

The reference to "*the romantic pains*" (rheumatic pains), is sufficient to make evident that "our age" refers to "old age." In fact, reference to an illness typical of old age, such as rheumatism, functions as a proper unequivocal gloss to the indexical expression "our age." Old age can account for health problems (Coupland & Coupland, 1994).

Lidia gives a detailed description of the therapies that are available from the doctor in question, *he does magnetotherapy does iontophoresis*, specifying the fees for the treatments, *for ten thousand liras one hour of magnetotherapy*. Moreover, she underlines the advantages of closeness and easy access to the therapy sessions, comparing this one to other therapy centers in town that are much more difficult to reach. Although in this case an association is made between the category "old" and its decremental character, a positive image of a knowledgeable, effective adult, able to look after her health and interests, is projected by this speaker. The image has nothing in common with the image of frailty and dependendence that we observed elsewhere (Taylor, 1992).

The requests for clarification in this dialogue construct the issue as relevant to the group. Lidia concludes by reproposing her initial idea of inviting the doctor to the Center, *if we ask him to come one day he will explain it to us.* Illness and its associated therapies are thus constructed as relevant issues to the institutional agenda of the Social Citizen Center, and the physician's presentation is proposed for inclusion in the Center's program of activities.

The physician's presentation appears to be halfway between an informative seminar (*he could . . . tell us about sickness concerning to tooo our age*) and a promotional initiative (*he will explain it to us*), a reference to the specific treatments that he provides in his ambulatory facility. Indirectly, the group is constructed by its own members as a potential market for private medical services (see Gilleard, 1996).

In contrast with the previous chapter, where positive identities were achieved by the older women mainly by differentiating themselves from the category "old," in the analysis here positive self-identifications are achieved by the women through association with the category "old" in relation to its institutional relevance. In fact, association with the category implies access to interesting institutionally designed activities and/or to special benefits and services.

The next section focuses on how specific institutional aims, procedures, and discourses are made relevant to the women in the course of their committee meetings and how these interfere with older women's definitions of the situation.

INSTITUTIONAL DEFINITIONS OF THE SUBJECT

Institutions not only have specific agendas, but also "needs" of their own that may have nothing to do with their functional aims: Their management and organization impose on members' attention issues that very often obscure the needs and priorities of the persons who are supposed to be attended to. This section illustrates how institutional "needs" and priorities assume a level of relevance greater than the older women's agendas and expectations.

In the next passage, a social worker introduces a new service that has just been established in the district, a center for menopause, what we could call "a gender- and age-specific institution":

Social worker:	I have still, a, message to give, (a different subject at three o'clock) it opens it was opened today for the first time this center for menopause [in San Marco
Berta:	[where where
Lidia:	oh! [this is something we wanted to hear about
Social worker:	[in San Marco
Lidia:	[( )
Social worker:	[(today)
Researcher:	[sss ssss
Social worker:	I chose you instead of going to participate in this opening,
Alma:	but where is it
Social worker:	so there is this center for menopause,
Alma:	yes
Social worker:	in San Marco,
Alma:	eh
Alba:	by now it is over for us
Alma:	[ssss
Social worker:	[in San Marco there is a gynecologist there are, three social workers,
Alma:	yes
Social worker:	I mean I too am in the, little group
	…
Lidia:	what are the characteristics of this center
Social worker:	well what are the characteristics of this center there is the possibility to have a gynecological visit, em with this doctor who is specializing in this sector when I say doctor I mean a gynecologist but she is a woman her name is ___, ___ and this possibility to have this medical examination, will then allow privileged routes, for the clinical examination in the hospital, because for the first time the local services will be in contact with the hospital in fact I'll be working inside the hospital with, ___ ___ I think this is his name who is the gynecologist who works in this sector, of menopause then meetings will be organized.

(2/22/94 Committee meeting of the Action Project)

The social worker introduces the news, *it was opened today for the first time this center for menopause,* welcomed by Lidia, *oh! this is something we wanted to hear about,* while Alma seeks an explanation, *but where is it,* and general

comments are expressed. In this way Lidia and Alma contribute to constructing the news as relevant to the group.

Alba's remarks, *by now it is over for us,* accurately correspond to the
medical reality for most of the women in the meeting, and are not picked
up by anyone. In this case the pro-term *us* is used to signal exclusion
(Watson, 1987). At the institutional level, menopause is defined as relevant
to older women, constructed as a homogenous group, by a powerful,
credible, and competent member: the social worker from the menopause
center, *there is a gynecologist there are three social workers . . . I mean I too am
in the, little group.* Members' relevancies are obscured, and this is particularly
evident in the description of the menopause center produced.

Lidia solicits information about the center, giving the social worker the
opportunity to point out its relevance to the women. This explanation,
though, is constructed around organizational structural problems: *For the
first time the local services will be in contact with the hospital.* In fact, the social
worker points out how the use of this center (*this possibility to have this medical
examination*) will facilitate access to further hospital examination (*will then
allow privileged routes, for the clinical examination in the hospital*). It is not clear
what needs on the part of the women could be answered, although there is
a reference to the organization of informational meetings (*there will be
meetings organized*). What is highlighted is not how the center could be useful
to the women, but how it can be used by the women from the standpoint
of organizational procedures; its relevance is taken for granted. It appears
as if the institution is useful in that it exists. In the next chapter we will see
this characteristic of institutions strategically used in arguments among
members of different institutions.

Just from this one passage, we can glimpse the immense institutional
machinery, particularly within the medical and caring system, hiding behind
the category "old." This machinery contributes to the definition of what
"being old" means in relation to powerful institutional practices and discourses. In the next transcript, institutional conflicts among two different
units of the Municipality of Perugia are made relevant to the women; also
in this case differences among women's and institutional "needs" are evident. It is the institutional ones that prevail.

Two departments of the Municipality of Perugia, the Equal Opportunity
Unit and the Social Services Unit, are discussed, and conflicts between
them are revealed in the course of this conversation in the committee
meeting. The topic of the conversation is the organization of an exhibition
of older people's work in which the older women's group will participate.
Lola is asking whether they are talking of the same exhibition being
organized by the Social Services Unit. Lola explains that she has just been
asked by an officer of the Social Services Unit to bring her poetry to an
exhibition:

Lola: is it the very one in the Commune? still this one
Officer: yes
Lola: or is it a different one
Officer: no (it is still that one at Rocca Paolina)
Lola: it is still this one, yes OK that one up there at the Commune (told me), if I could bring them to her, ( ) poetry and photos (on) the poster. That one at the Commune
Officer: but who who is she ((Lola turns around without replying)) but let's not make a muddle ladies ((with her voice slightly altered)) excuse me ladies here we are talking about the Action Project, ((background noise stops))
Lola: eh eh [(of the Project)
Officer: [well this work, this work that you were talking about of which you are talking about Lola, is it the work that you have done for the Action Project?
Lola: eh eh
Officer: and so if you (have done it) with the Action Project eh eh that to whom are you giving it [(what are they doing with it)
Lola: [it's said it was together ((turning towards Nina))
Nina: she wanted to bring it, to show it, at the Rocca Paolina
Officer: I understand it but you will bring it with all the things of the [Action Project
Nina: [and then you bring it with [all the things of the Action Project
Lola: [(but) this morning that lady at the Commune told me,
Officer: yes
Lola: [( )this thing that's why I am saying it
Nina: [( )listen to Irma ssss
Officer: since you have always participated in the Action Project haven't you? and so. Is this material the drawings the tales the poetry the photos or what it is for the Action Project [(we don't want to hang it)
Lola: [(certainly)
Officer: well but if you give it [(to the lady)
Lola: [(eh I know it) eh I found out just now that you were involved in it what can I know she told me this morning about it I don't know anything now another time, (that's why I was asking) explanations
Nina: well we solved it
(5/2/1994 Committee meeting of the Action Project)

With the question, *but who who is she*, the officer signals trouble, which is apparently understood as such by Lola who does not treat the question as a proper question by not answering it *((Lola turns around without replying))*. The officer makes explicit the trouble, *let's not make a muddle ladies*. The tone of her voice, *((with her voice slightly altered))*, together with the content of her words, produce immediate attention from the group, *((background noise stops))*.

The officer is now asking Lola to define the institutional attribution of her work, *is it the work that you have done for the Action Project?* Lola gives her assent, *he he*. Lola is made morally accountable (Silverman, 1993) for institutional ownership of her work. The officer's inarticulate remark, *and so if you (have done it) with the Action Project eh eh that to whom are you giving it*, signals the ordinariness, the commonsense facticity of her work belonging to the Action Project, and the moral sanctions implied in upsetting such order (Cuff & Payne, 1979). The institutional ownership of the women's work, which in the previous section was ambiguously conveyed, *we sent a bit of our things*, is here openly stated.

Nina attempts an explanation of Lola's intention, *she wanted to bring it, to show it, at the Rocca Paolina*. The officer twice underlines the importance of the institutional attribution of the older women's work, *I understand it but you will bring it with all the things of the Action Project; Is this material the drawings the tales the poetry the photos or what it is for the Action Project*. Lola feels the need to justify herself, *I found out just now that you were involved in it what can I know she told me this morning about it I don't know anything now another time*, and asserts her right to ask for explanation, *that's why I am saying it, (that's why I was asking) for explanations*. Both Nina and Lola contribute in this way to construct the moral accountability of the issue at hand.

The older women's work appears here to be constructed as an institutional possession. This is not a trivial issue. Institutions must be seen doing things; they do not only have to produce services, they must be seen performing them. They have to document their activities, make them visible, understandable, "witnessable," as a serious matter of social and political accountability. When Lola expresses her idea to offer her poetry for the Social Service Unit's exhibition, the officer expresses disagreement and anger. This is because the officer sees the risk that work carried out under the auspices of the Action Project will be credited to the Social Service Unit and not the Equal Opportunities Unit. But this issue is irrelevant to the women, who want mainly to see their works exhibited, as Nina explains it: *She wanted . . . to show it, at the Rocca Paolina*. Among the two relevancies, it is clearly the institutional one that prevails.

This interactional episode shows how specific institutional priorities, such as making the production of services publicly witnessable, are made relevant to the older women in the course of ordinary events. On the one hand, such institutional activities as the organization of the exhibition allows the women's work to be brought forward, thus producing positive and effective identities for them. On the other hand, institutional priorities establish the organization of the activity. Institutional aims and procedures are made relevant to the women, creating a different order of priorities. The institutional influence on the social production of identity is thus complex.

In this chapter, association with the category "old" has been highlighted in relation to its institutional relevance. Access to prestigious events, benefits, and services was implied in such association. In particular, institutionally organized activities can positively mobilize women's perceived spheres of action and life perspectives, adding new possibilities to what being an older woman can mean. In contrast to this positive institutional influence, however, the needs, priorities, procedures, and discourses that belong exclusively to specific institutional settings may impinge on older women's understanding and perception of issues and of the situation.

Institutional influence on the social process of identity production are developed at length in the next chapters, but already the complexity of such interrelations appears from the analysis of the preceding transcripts.

The next chapter looks at how gender identification is influenced by institutional discourses and practices. In particular, I examine transcripts that refer to the recurrent conflicts between the Equal Opportunity Unit and the Senior Citizen Centers during the 3 years of the Project. I show how the different institutional agendas had direct influence on the definition of space for the older women's initiatives and activities.

4

Institutional Conflicts
and Gender Identification

Institutions such as the Equal Opportunity Unit have changes in gender identity as part of their agenda; in fact, the proposition of new activities, roles, and responsibilities for women has a direct influence on identification processes, and is part of the aims and objectives of the institutional programs and projects. Discourses are generated by institution members that are relevant to identity production, as is shown in the following pages.

Chapter 3 showed some instances of the complex institutional influence on age identification processes. Relating to gender-relevant practices, institutional intervention is explicit and direct; it is part of the institutional aims of the Equal Opportunity Unit to promote activities that are innovative with regard to gender roles.

In this chapter I look at how, within the context of conflicts between two institutions (the Equal Opportunity Unit and the Senior Citizen Centers), specific discourses are used either to support and allow women's autonomous initiatives or to prevent and hinder them. This topic is further developed, showing how institutions are used as an "argument" in advocating autonomous women's initiatives.

The last part of the chapter presents some of the institutional initiatives of the Action Project that were particularly salient to gender identification processes.

CONFLICTS BETWEEN INSTITUTIONS

As already mentioned in the presentation of the history of the Action Project (see chapter 1), constant resistance was met at both institutional and personal levels by the women in carrying out the Action Project's initiatives. Resistance was offered by Senior Citizen Centers' members and presidents, Councillors of the Municipality of Perugia, and others. Some features of these conflicts are illustrated in this chapter, pointing out the meanings they had for the women involved.

TALKING INSTITUTIONS

The following transcript reports a long and complex strip of interaction in which different institutions are brought into being in the course of the discussion and power conflicts among them are made evident. It is part of a quite animated session. In fact, four presidents of Senior Centers and a few other male members arrived unexpectedly at the first committee meeting of the Action Project after the summer break in 1992. They had not been invited, nor had they announced their intention to attend. The conversation excerpted herein is constructed around the ambiguous characterization of the subjects on the base of their institutional or gender membership.

This first meeting of the season was audiotaped. Because I was not involved in videotaping, I was able to participate fully in the discussion, as is noticeable by my long contribution. (See the prologue, where I explain my double role as observer [researcher] and participant [facilitator of the Action Project], and the first chapter, where the analytical treatment of such data is pointed out.)

The president of the Senior Center in San Sisto, a suburb of Perugia, is now referring to problems that had emerged the previous year in the course of conducting of the Senior Center's activities.

President:	Let's not repeat, some mistakes that were made last year, not really mistakes but anyway, there was a certain disagreement, here we all have to get on well together, we as are umm the Action Project is developed inside, the Community Centers, isn't it? and undoubtedly, we, do not want to [lose, our autonomy
Woman:	[( )
President:	because we, as the Socio-cultural Community Center in San Sisto have activities with middle school, with primary school, with the ( ) undoubtedly we don't want to lose, these initiatives that we have, to collaborate together with the Action Project, but we don't have to create two separate things because otherwise we really find ourselves [quarrelling quarrelling again,
Woman:	[( )
President:	[because there are things
Researcher:	[not separate according to me excuse me, if you have finished I'd like to make a basic clarification,
President:	yes
Researcher:	in order, to understand the spirit of the Project, that is the basic idea of the Project, for which a proposal was made at EC and it was funded by [EC by

President:	[by EC, but I know that
Researcher:	umm by the department of Equal Opportunities and, by Social Affairs, it was mainly because of, it must be clear that it is a Project based on women's initiatives, now this doesn't mean that men cannot [participate,
Woman:	[(no because they are them too) (whispering))
Researcher:	because in fact in all the activities singing, [the various activities,
Woman:	[( )
Researcher:	men take part too, but it must be clear that, the management of the Project, the Project is conducted, is carried out by women it is a women's initiative because otherwise the very function, of the Project [is distorted that is
President:	[I wouldn't like, dear Elisabetta that we end up looking on we are
Researcher:	[no
President:	[the spectators =
Researcher:	= that is =
President:	= we have a managing committee, there are other members
Researcher:	[that is
President:	[undoubtedly the greater number,
Woman:	[( ) there are men too
President:	of elderly people are women we agree on that, for goodness' sake, eh equal opportunity undoubtedly means um men and women and [there are some men,
Woman:	[certainly
President:	but
Officer:	yes (in fact)
Researcher:	[that is I would say
Officer:	[Rino
President:	[um the management is yours but we also have to do something because [otherwise ( )
Researcher:	[within the activities within [the activities it is very clear
Officer:	[no we don't do everything Rino, Rino this is only the Action Project it is not the [Socio-cultural Center
Woman:	[Socio-cultural Center
Officer:	of San Sisto [nor of Monte Grillo nor anything
President:	[but the elements the subjects where are they within the social Centers well [we don't but nobody rejects the Action Project in the least
Officer:	[this those that joined those that joined
President:	for goodness' sake,

Officer: no [but for
President: [I am the first one, [to say that we need this
Officer: [no but in fact here let's clarify [let's
simply clarify
Researcher: [yes
in fact
Officer: the Action Project is only a part, of the activities, and that's it
therefore then, in any Center you can do two thousand other
activities and in fact you do them you have juuuust listed them
don't you you do two thousand other activities, that belong to
the Senior Center this is the activity that is, also, developed inside
the Senior Centers, but it is, decided and managed by women,
anybody who wants to everybody can participate, but the decisions the decisions are up to the women because it is a reflection
on women's condition, in the third age
(9/10/92 Committee meeting of the Action Project)

The president of the Senior Center starts by pointing out the need for autonomous initiative by the Senior Centers, *we, do not want to lose, our autonomy*. He renders explicit the "organizational references" (Sacks, 1992; Watson, 1987) of the pro-terms "we," *we, as the Socio-cultural Community Center in San Sisto*. Then he lists some of the activities carried out by the Center, underlining that, *we don't want to lose, these initiatives that we have*, implicitly indicating a threat to their institutional autonomy. The participa- tion in the Action Project does not have to mean either carrying out separate initiatives, *to collaborate together with the Action Project, but we don't have to create two separate things*. This is indicated as a possible cause of recurring disagreements, *we really find ourselves quarrelling quarrelling again*.

On the one hand, the President is advocating autonomy for the Center's activities; on the other hand, he is advocating joint activity with the Action Project (institutionally speaking that is the Equal Opportunity Unit of the Municipality of Perugia). This seems contradictory, unless "separate things" is understood in terms of gender differentiation of activities. This ambiguity, as we will see, is built into the subsequent turns at talk which re-propose the two competing interpretations.

The researcher's turn at talk overlaps the president's; she signals her intervention as an interruption (Makri-Tsilipakou, 1994; Murata, 1994; West & Zimmerman, 1985), attempting to repair it, *excuse me, if you have finished*. The repetition of *"separate,"* projects current turn-at-talk content on the explanation of this term, and it is focused on the issue of gender differentiation of activities. A further projection is provided, qualifying the relevance of the issue at hand, *I'd like to make a basic clarification . . . in order, to understand the spirit of the Project*.

Before specifying the nature of the project, *the Project is conducted, is carried out by women it is a women's initiative,* the researcher refers to the institutionally guaranteed status of the Project in a rather lengthy way, *for which a proposal was made at the EC and it was funded by the EC by . . . department of Equal Opportunities and, by Social Affairs.* This legitimatizes the very existence of the activity distinction based on gender. She also specifies that the distinction refers only to the management of such activities not participation, *now this doesn't mean that men cannot participate . . . because in fact in all the activities singing, the various activities . . . men take part too.*

The president interrupts the researcher's turn by referring to his fear of losing autonomy over decision making, *I wouldn't like, dear Elisabetta that we end up to be looking on to be . . . the spectators.* Again, the ambiguity in the use of the pro-terms is reproposed: "We" refers to the institution, the Senior Center, *we have a managing committee.* But as well, it refers to the membership category "male," *there are other members.* That "other" refers to males is made clear from the specification that follows, *undoubtedly the greater number, of elderly people are women.* Then the president explains the meaning of equal opportunity matters as guaranteeing male presence as well as women's, *equal opportunity undoubtedly means um men and women and there are some men,* reversing the priorities in the issue.

In the meantime, a real battle for the floor is going on: The researcher tries to get a turn and she manages to insert half a sentence at the fourth attempt, while the officer is also trying to gain one. It sounds like an institutional struggle for dominance as well as for gender dominance.

The officer's use of the president's first name, *Rino,* and her expression of support, *yes (in fact),* to his rather provocative definition of equal opportunities, can be explained by her conciliatory effort. She proposes an interpretation of the "quarrel" as a matter of definition of institutional spheres of action, *no we don't do everything Rino, Rino this is only the Action Project it is not the Socio-cultural Center . . . of San Sisto nor of Monte Grillo nor anything;* that is, the Action Project's activities are few among the many activities that are carried out by Senior Centers' members, *the Action Project is only a part, of the activities.* Then she addresses the second term of the ambiguity, that is the reference to the membership category "male," re-stating the main issues proposed by the researcher, *it is, decided and managed by women, anybody who wants to everybody can participate, but the decisions the decisions belong to the women because it is a reflection on women's condition.*

In this piece of conversation the competition among institution for the definition of their respective fields of action fade into gender dominance issues. The president's discourse uses ambiguity to propose a bind that practically negates space to women's independent initiatives. In fact, he wants autonomous action for the Senior Center, but does not want separate activities conducted through the Action Project. Similar discourses recur in the data.

In this case, the bind is resolved by the joint researcher and officer's interventions, effectively advocating a space for women's initiatives. First, they point out the limited number of Action Project initiatives, because the activities promoted by the Action Project represent only a small portion of those carried out in the Centers. Second, gender segregation of activities refers only to their management. Third, they point out the significance of such initiatives using the very existence of institutions and legislation on equal opportunities as an argument to ratify their importance. Other examples of this type of argument are reported in the next section.

Here it is evident how the discourse on equal opportunities is used in quite polarized ways: to guarantee women's participation in decision making, and to insure men's participation. As Foucault wrote: "We must conceive discourse as a series of discontinuous segments whose tactical function is neither uniform nor stable" (Foucault, 1978, p. 100). Discourses are generated, circulated, transformed (Duranti & Goodwin, 1992). They have no fixed meaning; they can be twisted and argued against in such a way as to serve opposite cause (Foucault, 1978), as occurs in this case.

A power struggle among institutional participants is carried out through the actual development of discourses that can be read as a sequence of strategic moves in reciprocally defining institutional space.

Institutional struggles like the one being analyzed here have an impact on women's lives, in particular, on their participation in the Senior Citizen Centers. For example, shortly after this episode, participation in the Action Project was withdrawn by the Senior Citizen Center of San Sisto until a new president was elected. In the following transcript I examine how such conflicts are perceived by the women.

WOMEN'S COMPLAINTS: BEING HEARD

The issues raised by the women, in the discussion that immediately followed the one just reported, refer to problems of communication and, more precisely, to access to decision making in relation to Senior Citizen Centers' initiatives.

A short while after the four Senior Center presidents left, the conversation continued on the same topic. In the following excerpt, Rita is commenting on the issue raised by the president of the Senior Center of San Sisto, starting with a self-reprimand:

    Rita: well these things though we too who are delegates, myself first, we had to clarify well that it is a thing, ahm still belonging to the Center owned by women but yet connected to the Center, because naturally, I can understand them too those who feel a bit excluded, we were saying that [(last year)

Nina: [(I was saying at the beginning) ((some women talk among themselves))

Rita: because maybe they didn't understand well, since the beginning, how this thing is [this thing

Nina: [but why, we, took on the organization of the Action Project, because (sometimes) if [you notice,

Researcher: [excuse me if we don't speak one at a time

Nina: the men were always saying let's do this let's do that and we would run after them like sheep now that we have taken a bit of the initiative they feel. [(Annoyed in my opinion)

Rita: [(then also last year we attended these meetings and then we talked about them, nobody would listen to us ((some people talking together))

Women: sssss

Aldo: this happened, that we started out all together then, the Women's Project came out and then everything changed, [(   ) it was

Rita: no   [(   )

Researcher: but Nina is saying that when you put women and men together the those who decide are always the men
            . . .

Lidia: (should) understand that also when we came here to the meetings [not

Rita: [we didn't always report ((many people speaking at once))

Lidia: eh [(   )

Officer: [but there is this problem, in some Centers there is we know that there is I really don't know [why it is so

Rita: [but Mrs. Irma we (have reported) but they don't listen to us=

Lidia: =they took it lightly they took it that they didn't give it any weight I don't know why=

Rita: =because we are women=

Lidia: =I, I refer to our eh,

Rita: because we are women she's gone to have fun she's gone to the meeting but what happened at the meeting?
            (9/10/92 Committee meeting of the Action Project)

The men's feelings of exclusion, *I can understand them too those who feel a bit excluded,* are attributed by Rita to the Action Project delegates' inability to communicate decisions in such a form as to render them part of the Senior Center activities, *we had to clarify well that it is a thing, ahm still belonging to the Center owned by women but yet connected to the Center.*

Nina disagrees with Rita and explains the question in terms of power: male dominance, *the men were always saying let's do this let's do that and we would run after them like sheep.* Further, she suggests that the men are threatened by the women's initiatives, *now that we took a bit of the initiative they feel. (Annoyed in my opinion).* At this point Rita changes her self-reproach into an accusation of not having been being listened to, *last year we attended these meetings and then we talked about them, nobody would listen to us,* thus apparently agreeing with Nina.

Aldo, a male member who had not left the room, points out how the Women's Project brought division to their group, *we started out all together then, the Women's Project came out and then everything changed.* The researcher's objection, *when you put women and men together those who decide are always the men,* is then developed at length by both the researcher and the Equal Opportunity officer in a dialogue that is not included in the preceding transcript.

Lidia and Rita repropose the problem as one of not being heard (Spender, 1980). This fragment of conversation is impressive: At a first hearing it appeared to me to be a single-person intervention, but a closer listening showed it to be the result of Lidia and Rita collaborating in a perfectly synchronized manner, weaving together their conversation. Such forms of talk among women have been described already by Morgenthaler (1990), who pointed out:

> The members did not seem to be conducting some sort of verbal wrestling in which neither could truly win the floor. On the contrary, they seemed finely tuned, highly organized, and entirely cooperative. (p. 547)

These women are not only commenting on the fact of not being heard but are producing what being heard means to them, that is a collaborative and a highly supportive form of talk. This stream of conversation communicates affiliation through its very form of production (see Sacks, 1992, p. 145).

In the interchange, their awareness of women's autonomous activity being discredited is noticeable, *they took it lightly they took it that they didn't give it any weight; she's gone to have fun she's gone to the meeting,* and the reason is explicitly attributed to gender membership, *because we are women.* Gender identification appears to have concrete negative implications for the women, including not being heard and difficulties in taking part in decision making.

I further explore the issue of women's complaints about not being heard in chapter 5. Through the analysis of some transcripts taken from a Senior Center committee meeting, I intend to focus on the decision-making process in two Senior Citizen Centers in order to highlight discourses and practices that either block or facilitate women's participation. Now, however, I turn to a transcript in which the conflicts between institutions (Senior Citizen Centers and Equal Opportunity Units) are further developed, reporting part of the speech in which the Equal Opportunity's councillor openly attacks the president of the Senior Citizen Center of San Sisto.

INSTITUTIONAL ATTACK

In the following transcript of a committee meeting, which was convened in November 1992, the councillor for the Equal Opportunity Unit partici-pated, starting the meeting by strongly criticizing the Senior Citizen Centers' presidents who were hindering the Action Project. Such a direct attack represents a rather unusual political move. It also provides a clear yet provocative understanding of the seriousness of the conflict involving the Senior Citizen Centers' presidents in the preceding committee meeting of the Action Project. The passage by the councillor offers a further costruction of older women: They are portrayed as heroines.

The councillor has just initiated the meeting. The following transcript comes afterwards and is a good example of politicians' verbosity. The resulting speech is easy to hear because of the oral stresses distributed appropriately across the speech that call audience attention to specific focal words (unfortunately, these are lost in the transcript); but it is not always logically coherent or clearly understandable, as is evident in the written text. (For this reason the translation into English was unusually difficult.)

Councillor: I am saying if this call us all towards taking responsibility for commitment, and individual and collective work, well this pre-cisely should, make us consider, too on the fact that all a series, let's say of institution of structures for services, that also this reality, of the elderly condition don't they they materialized I mean, in our Borough territory well they should also be invested always more and better eeeh, they should realize to be clear to understand the importance, a bit of the effort that we decided to undertake, eh with this Action Project, therefore on our side, as Office, as Council for the Equal Opportunity, we have already in our calendar a series of let's say of political initiatives, institu-tional ones, that we want to realize because, for example (larger) institutions also, of our town, and of our region, there could be

full awareness of the importance of our Project, and so, emm an attitude of cooperation too, in this perspective we intend I intend to organize also, a series of meetings in some way at an institutional level with the same Region and the same Province of Perugia in order to bring to these administrators, of the essence of the choice of merit that we did with our Project. You can understand that, just this is important because there is also, a a a desire a will I believe this is, right of a, to be representative, to the discussion and the research therefore also of the attention from larger Institutions I mean, of the Borough, uum
(10/9/92 Committee meeting of the Action Project)

The councillor announces her intention to promote political initiatives to make the Action Project known to other local administrative bodies, *we intend I intend to organize also, a series of meetings in some way at an institutional level with the same Region and the same Province of Perugia.* Notice the shift from the institutional pro-term "we," that is "speaking in one's organizational capacity" (Watson, 1987), to the personal pro-term "I": The institution here is incarnated.

In expressing the aims of these meetings the councillor is constructing the Action Project as meriting the attention of larger institutions, *they should realize to be clear to understand the importance, a bit of the effort that we decided to undertake, eh with this Action Project.* A grading of institutional importance is projected by the use of the comparative, *larger Institutions I mean, of the Borough.* The Equal Opportunity Unit as well as the Senior Citizen Centers are framed within a classification of institutions as more or less important.

The councillor then continues by focusing on the conflict with the Senior Citizen Centers:

Councillor: perhaps we'd be proud I don't know if we are proud, I don't believe it because I believe that we are all together repositories of a proposal and a socio-political and cultural initiative, that I mean it has a sign, it is visible, eem, it is meeting the consent of a lot of women, a lot of realities and services exactly that I mean, are interested in the life of older people, here too with some negative exceptions and that it is unpleasant to have to notice and to underline, it doesn't depend either, on us or on you it depends probably a bit on the individual, personal and political short-sightedness of who doesn't want to understand this experience here I want to talk very clearly, and I refer to the attitude of some luckily it seems to me that they are a bit a minority but there are some Seniors Centers through their chairs the Center eem the Social Center, for elderly people of San Sisto is emblematic

in this respect it seems to me that it gives space in my opinion to an attitude that it's completely incomprehensible, unacceptable, and absolutely short-sighted in every respect, I believe by the way that exactly the women who take part in these Social Centers the same Social Center (I mean) of San Sisto, will certainly be able because they are the protagonists of some of the experiences, to assert, their experience and their choice, also towards their collegues who go to that Center, we are women we are women and many of us of course or rather every one of us fought her own life, she was able to live it, often really, eem suffering fighting experiencing pain and rejoice therefore I don't believe that any of us is afraid, of the attitude more or less short-sighted more or less, not very democratic that somebody eventually, could adopt that in everyone of us everyone of you also, the strength if you believe also in the work in the initiative that we have started, to be able to convince also the associations in your own territory, your colleagues men and women, of the importance also for each one of you if of course this is important to go on and continue his experience
(10/9/92 Committee meeting of the Action Project)

The strong, direct attack on the Senior Citizen Centers, *there are some Seniors Centers through their chairs the Center eem the Social Center, for elderly people of San Sisto is emblematic in this respect . . . to an attitude that it's completely incomprehensible, unacceptable, and absolutely short-sighted in every respect,* is embedded in this institutional grading and the Senior Citizen Centers clearly reside at the bottom of the list. The expression of general acceptance met by the Action Project, *it is meeting the consent of a lot of women, a lot of realities and services exactly that I mean, are interested in the life of older people,* is used to construct the resistance expressed from some Senior Citizen Centers as truly unreasonable.

The councillor clearly expresses a distinction between the institutional body, the Senior Citizen Centers, and the personal attitudes of the Centers' chairs, *it depends probably a bit on the individual, personal and political short-sightedness of who doesn't want to understand this experience.* The distinction is used to minimize the meaning of such resistance, portraying it as exceptional and idiosyncratic.

Nevertheless, what is noteworthy about this resistance is its rhetorical use by the councillor to build connection with her audience. First, there is the expression of personal feelings, as evident in *perhaps we'd be proud* or *I don't believe that any of us is afraid.* Second, there is the exhortation to the women to fight, again calling on feelings, *suffering fighting experiencing pain and rejoice.*

Here the women are constructed as heroines, *we are women we are women and many of us of course or rather every one of us fought her own life, she was able to live it.* They are heroines who are called to undertake another deed, *to be able to convince also the associations in your own territory, your colleagues men and women, of the importance . . . to go on and continue this experience.*

What is seen by the female project participants as an interactional problem bound to gender membership and male dominance, becomes transformed by the councillor into an institutional conflict between the Equal Opportunity Unit and some Senior Citizen Centers. Institutional aims, practices, and conflicts become gender relevant, with immediate consequences for the women's lives: their participation in decision making, and exclusion from or inclusion in activities, for example.

To summarize, the resistance to the Action Project initiatives generated various strategies and discourses in an attempt to contrast and accommodate such opposition. Particularly recurrent and significant in the discussions is the use of the existence of institutions and legislation for equal opportunities as an argument to sustain the right and importance of women's initiatives and leadership. In the first section, for example, it was shown how the researcher highlighted the institutional sponsorship of the Action Project as a way to ratify it. I develop this topic further in the next section; it is a rather indirect influence of institutions on the process of identification, although it is quite powerful, it is a symbolic influence.

INSTITUTIONS AS "ARGUMENTS"

The conflicts between the Senior Citizen Centers and the Equal Opportunity Unit were produced, made relevant, and made accountable through a series of concrete problems in the members' conduct of ordinary activities. Communication difficulties, episodes of miscommunication and withdrawal of information, were frequent. The decision to videotape some of the Senior Citizen Centers' managing committee meetings was in part motivated by the intention to verify the forms of communication between the Action Project and the Centers. Of particular interest was the type of information on the Action Project initiatives reported by the women who were members of the managing committees in their Centers. Problems of communication were a constant concern and a frequent topic of discussion in the committee meetings.

Prior to the following transcript, the officer had posed the problem of how the decisions, initiatives, and activities of the Action Project are reported in the Centers, in order to ascertain whether more structured forms of communication are necessary. Lidia is now commenting on the problem of resistance towards the Project. Discussion develops on the institutional attribution of women's activities:

Lidia: there is this dichotomy ((background wispering))
Lidia: between, [Action Project and the Cultural Centers, or for
Nina: [ssss. [Of course of course
Lidia: [Senior Citizens or how you prefer to call them, there this real Berlin wall (   ) and that we should make it (crumble). And this wall in my opinion was built, for a specific purpose from some people it was used a bit this will to put one against each other, who takes part in the women's project is one thing, the Senior Citizens Centers [is another
Nina: ((nodding)) [is another ((all talking at once))
Officer: since this interpretation came out at times [at times
Woman: [(   )
Officer: so, they say who works for the Action Project does not work for the Senior Citizen Center
Ida: [no no and why?
Ilda: [no no for both
Officer: but what do you ((gesture with her hands meaning "what does it mean")) nooo but it has nothing to do with working for both [the Action Project, is the Borough=
Nina: [together. =All together
Ilda: and then (still Center)
Officer: the Senior Citizen Center was created by the Borough.
Ilda: eh eh eh, [eh eh eh
Officer: it (was   [   ) by the Borough,
Ida: that's right
Officer: what one does, for the Action Project, in Monte Grillo is Monte Grillo's work,
Ida: that's right
Officer: for the Action Project, what one does in Ponte Felcino, for the Action Project ((Ilda nods)) but for the Action Project it does not mean, for, the Equal Opportunity Unit and therefore (not for the Center) ((gesture with her hand meaning from left to right "never"))
Nina: [(that's enough)
Ilda: [nooo (   )
Officer: [no it is (the program of the) Center
           (5/2/93 Committee meeting of the Action Project)

Lidia points out how the women are put in a position of choice between two different institutional affiliations, *who takes part in the women's project is one thing, the Senior Citizens Centers is another.* Note that the term *women's project* corresponds in Italian to the name of the Equal Opportunity Unit, "Progetto Donna." On various occasions, though, it was used to indicate the Action Project. Here the meaning is ambiguous. In any case, the conflict is clearly expressed in reference to different institutions.

The words *one* and *other*, in the expression, *one against each other*, in Italian are feminine; therefore they refer in particular to a contrapositioning among the women in the Centers, which, according to Lidia, has been purposely created, *this wall in my opinion was built, for a specific purposes from some people it was used a bit this will to put one against each other.*

Ilda proposes a solution that sees the women participating in the initiative of both the Senior Citizen Centers and the Action Project, *for both.* The officer decisively contrasts this perspective of contraposition and the solution offered by Ilda, *it has nothing to do with working for both.* She points out that both the Action Project and the Senior Citizen Centers are an emanation of the Borough, *the Action Project, is the Borough . . . the Senior Citizen Center was created by the Borough.* Recall that the Centers were officially asked by the Equal Opportunities Unit to take part in the Action Project. The Action Project initiatives must be considered an integral part of the Senior Citizen Centers' program, *what one does, for the Action Project, in Monte Grillo is Monte Grillo's work . . . for the Action Project.*

Structural features of institutions are used by the officer as an argument to fight the hostility and resistance met by the women in the Centers; the Centers, being an outgrowth of the Borough, are given a subsidiary institutional status. At the same time, the Action Project, being a Borough initiative, is used as an argument to ratify its value and importance.

The officer goes on to explain, *for the Action Project it does not mean, for, the Equal Opportunity Unit . . . no it is (the program of the) Center.* She seems to be contradicting herself, in that the Equal Opportunity Unit is part of the Borough and the one part promoting the Action Project. In fact, what she points out is the clear attribution of the women's activities as belonging to the Centers, that is that women's initiative has to be considered an integral part of the Centers' activities. This was the Equal Opportunity Unit's main agenda in establishing the Action Project—a point made present, argued for, and activated in and through this dispute.

Institutions, or more precisely institutional members, not only produce actions and discourses that have a powerful influence on identity processes; institutions have a symbolic power that can be strategically employed in interaction. We have seen here how their very existence and their structural composition are used as arguments to ratify the Action Project initiatives and sustain women's initiatives and leadership in the Centers. The discourse of the significance of the Action Project, of women's initiatives, is made relevant to the women through the reference to institutional support of such a Project. This use of institutions for the purpose of argument recurs in the data.

CREATING A SPACE FOR WOMEN

The previous sections have illustrated how institutional conflicts fade into gender contrapositioning and have a direct effect on identification processes. Also, I have shown how institutions are used symbolically in advocating a space for women's initiatives. In this section, I briefly illustrate some specific features of the Project having a direct impact on gender identification processes and how these contributed specifically to redrawing the older women's self-images and identities.

WHAT THE PROJECT MEANS TO THE WOMEN

As I pointed out in chapter 1, singing and theater workshops, as well as other Action Project initiatives, were very effective in attracting women to the Centers. This occurred despite the perception that these were mainly a "male" space. On many occasions, either in the interviews during the pilot research (Paoletti, 1997c) or in the course of various committee meetings, the women expressed their enthusiasm for the Action Project and how their lives had changed by participating in it. These themes are explored in the remainder of this chapter.

The following passage is part of the discussion of the evaluation of a singing performance that was reported in chapter 2. Sara has just expressed her disagreement with excluding people from the singing group. She is now telling how her participation in the singing group, as well as in other Action Project initiatives, is important for her life:

> Sara: for me that's I am, it's a short while that I go to the Center for the Elderly of Villa Pitignano (but) it's a beautiful experience, also because, I did never go out, I didn't, nothing I, home and work let's say (up until now) now I found, this place where to go, I enjoy it very much a really beautiful, experience I never came to the Town Hall, on the 10th I went was it the 10th?
>
> Ida: yes
> Officer: yes
> Sara: for me it was a fabulous thing,

Woman: [( )
 Sara: [yes, really, and I'll remember it and if I can.
  Ida: that's it
 Sara: I'll always come ((clapping))
         (12/18/92 Committee meeting of the Action Project)

As a woman, Sara sees access to public places as severely restricted, *I did never go out, I didn't, nothing I, home and work* (Paoletti, 1997c). She cannot just go out, she needs a place to go to, *now I found, this place where to go.* Moreover she describes the public meeting, when the singing performance took place, as *a fabulous thing.* In particular, she underlines that *I never came to the Town Hall* (the meeting was held in a splendid frescoed medieval hall). The applause that follows her intervention constructs her experience as exemplary, that is, shared by the group (M. J. Atkinson, 1984).

The participation in the Action Project represented a decisive improvement in the quality of life for many women. In some cases this had a positive consequence for their health. Social contacts, new friendships, and interesting things to do were the most obvious changes causing an improvement, but the Action Project aimed to act at a deeper level: It promoted women's initiatives and leadership. It is to the treatment of this topic that I now turn.

WOMEN'S INITIATIVES AND LEADERSHIP

Above all, the Action Project initiatives tend to focus on women's interests, preferences, and priorities. In particular, in the theater workshop, the choice of topics tended to privilege women's experience, and as a result women were given leading roles in the actual performance. For example, the work "The Rice-Weeder" was based on the real-life experience of one of the women who, in her youth, had worked in the rice fields; another one of the "Little Stories of Everyday Life" presents the difficulties of a tired grandmother who has to clean the house and look after the offspring of her children, leaving no time for herself. The grandmother's fairy tale tells the story of a grandmother who has lost her nephew. While looking for him, she has lots of adventures. A very unconventional image of a grandmother is portrayed: active, creative, and enterprising.

The next transcript is taken from a working session of this fairy tale's performance. The grandmother is now back in her past, with her old friends, playing one of her favorite games, "Queen, little queen," which consists of arriving first at the queen's castle, asking directions of the queen. In the analysis, it will be shown how women's leading role is made a matter of course by choosing a girl's game.

Teacher:	queen little queen, go
Elio:	queen little queen how how many steps should I make to come to your castle
Tecla:	two like a giant
Teacher:	well excuse me but, it cannot be casual every time,
Ida:	of course
Teacher:	[( ) every time
Ida:	[(we'd say it precisely)
Teacher:	no every time it must be the same person, who starts then let's say that since you don't remember it (well because) they were female games they were female games [(so)
Ida:	[((laughes)) put a woman instead
Teacher:	Nilde,
Nilde:	eh
Teacher:	do you know that the
Nilde :	( )
Teacher:	then immediately, queen little queen, you are always the first one (1/25/93 Theater workshop at Montegrillo)

Because the teacher has not given precise guidelines, Elio, the only man among five women in the scene, takes the initiative and starts the game, *queen little queen how how many steps should I make to come to your castle*. Tecla, who is the queen, validates Elio's move, giving indication of the steps to be performed in order to reach the castle, *two like a giant*.

The teacher intervenes, *it cannot be casual every time*, in order to give specific guidelines. Ida's saying, *(we'd say it precisely)*, shows her understanding of "casual" as referring to the words of the game; in this way, she shows that she has noticed a mistake. The teacher signals disagreement, *no*, and specifies what she means, *every time it must be the same person*, but then she also points out a mistake in the words, *since you don't remember it (well)* and attributes the cause to gender membership, designating the game as a category-bound activity (Sacks, 1992), *(because) they were female games*.

Ida highlights the inadequacy of Elio's intervention with levity and humor, *((laughes)) put a woman instead*; while the teacher asks a woman to start the game, *you are always the first one*, after ascertaining that she knows the words, *do you know that*. This ordinary occurrence shows how the focus on female experience (female games, in this case) allows the construction of women's centrality as a matter of course, without apparently creating any contrasts or conflicts.

Thus, women are not only given access to a variety of previously unknown activities through the Action Project, but their knowledge, experience, and concerns are brought forward and placed at the center of attention. Here women can experience new, diverse, and positive encounters and identities. Beyond this, the main goal of the Action Project was to encourage women's participation in decision making at all levels in their communities. Moreover, it offered the women a space to start to perceive themselves as justified and capable of assuming managerial and leadership roles in their communities. These were explicit institutional objectives of the Action Project.

To summarize this chapter, some features of institutional influence on the processes of gender identification were explored. I showed how institutional conflicts over defining respective fields of action affected the women, broadening or restricting spaces for their autonomous initiatives. I highlighted the symbolic use of institutions in argumentative strategies, showing how the appeal to the very existence of certain institutions is used to ratify relevant practices and convince the women of their importance. In fact, the existence of these institutions becomes a resource for members to call on in debate.

From the analysis so far, identity appears as an ongoing production, managed in the course of interactions, in and through the conduct of ordinary activities. Not only personal, but institutional, agendas have an influence on the processes of identity production. Institutional influences on identity production processes appear to be intricate and multiform.

The next chapter focuses the analysis on the communication processes in the managing committee meetings of two Senior Citizen Centers, exploring further the problem expressed by the women of not being heard. In it, I highlight differences among women's communicational skills. I aim primarily to point out how specific members' skills, drive, and perspectives, in short—their projected personal identities—have an influence on the production of specific features of institutions.

5

Members' Personal Identities
and Institutions

The previous chapters have explored various features of institutional discourses and activities relevant to age and gender identification. Particularly in chapter 4, I have pointed out how institutional conflicts between the Senior Citizen Center and the Equal Opportunity Unit were salient in determining spaces for the women's autonomous initiatives. Recurrent communication problems were pointed out, together with the various strategies and discourses produced by members in dealing with them.

Communication problems are further explored in this chapter, through the analysis of some transcripts from the managing committee meetings of two Senior Citizen Centers. I look at how resistance to women's autonomous initiatives, as well as different modalities of communication, are produced in the course of conducting the ordinary business during the meetings. Different levels of resistance, as well as differences in communication skills of two women participating in the Centers' committees, are highlighted.

In this chapter I aim primarily to point out how communication skills or other relevant aspects of personal identities influence particular features of the institutions of which the individuals are members. I think that it is methodologically and theoretically relevant to point out the circularity and interconnection between identity production processes and the enactment of institutions by members. In fact, this issue is central to understanding processes of change as well as instances of social reproduction. I begin by examining how communication problems were discussed in the committee meetings of the Action Project.

COMMUNICATION PROBLEMS

Before looking at the interaction within the managing committee of the Centers relating to their communication problems with the women's group, I present an example of how such issues are made relevant to the women, and their point of view on the matter. The following transcript reports the continuation of the evaluation of the diffusion of information about the Action Project activities in the Centers. As stressed in chapter 4, discussions on this topic recur in the data. The officer is now illustrating various possible modalities of communication:

Officer: just to go back to the communication in the Centers, very well, who is part of the committee of the Action Project and then she (gives back) speaks [in their Centers

Ilda: [of course we tell about it

Ida: ((nodding)) [of course

Officer: [there's instead who tell a little bit to who asks them or aaah eeh

Ida: yes eh. [( )

Women: [( )

Officer: [or she tells (to somebody she meets on the street) at the moment but, I say, apart from this. Is it possible to think of some other form of communication that could be more how could I say [clearer

Woman: [( )

Officer: eeem more uummm concrete that's it [( )

Women: [( )

Researcher: [regular

Nina: we finally have been admitted into the managing committee, the committee of our Center and they invited the women of the Action Project [they invited us to participate

Officer: [ohOOO!!!! ((she smiles taking her arms down indicating "at last!"))

Nina: ((laughs)) in the next meeting of the committee there'll be three or four women going to, [good

Women: [( )

Nina: yes. Finally

Lidia: the committee of the District

Nina: no no the committeee of our Social Center

Lidia: ah! why, weren't you in the committee?

Nina: no no no.

Lidia: [ah no you didn't

Woman: [( )

Nina: they never invited us Irma was always saying you must get an invitation if you need to tell them something mustn't you, therefore I used to tell them but Rino at a certain point has even,

	done he stopped with the Action Project therefore (you see) it was that bad [wasn't it
Woman:	[( )
Nina:	now, our new president invited us officially
	(2/5/93 Committee meeting of the Action Project)

The officer presents different methods of spreading information about the Action Project, *speaks in their Centers; who tell a little bit to who asks them; she tells (to somebody she meets on the street)*; these are considered more or less informal. She then questions whether there is a need for more structured methods of information, *other form of communication that could be more how could I say clearer . . . concrete.* The researcher adds, *regular.* In doing so the officer and the researcher are jointly constructing the communication among the Project and the Centers as being problematic, lacking, and random.

At the initial mention of the problem, Ilda and Ida confirm their commitment to communicating news to their Center in Monte Grillo, *of course we tell about it; ((nodding)) of course.* On the other hand, Nina reports exciting news, *we finally have been admitted into the managing committee . . . of our Center and they invited the women of the Action Project they invited us to participate.* This news is met by an exclamation of relief and satisfaction by the officer, *ohOOO!!!! ((she smiles taking her arms down indicating "at last!")).* Considering that in most of the Centers' managing committees the vast majority of members are male, *there'll be three or four women going,* is certainly reportable as good news, as Nina says, *good.*

Lidia, by asking for clarification, *ah! why, weren't you in the committee,* and by repeating Nina's answer, *ah no you didn't,* constructs the fact of the latter's nonparticipation as noticeable, that is, unusual and strange, therefore requiring an explanation, while implicitly conveying that she herself is a member of the committee for her Center. Nina provides the solicited explanation and points out the problems she previously encountered at the Center. She emphasizes *they never invited us,* even when she asked to talk to the committee, *I used to tell them*; in fact, the officer is said to have encouraged her to do so, *Irma was always saying you must get an invitation if you need to tell them something.* The president of the Center at San Sisto arrived at the point of officially withdrawing support for the Action Project, *Rino at a certain point . . . stopped with the Action Project . . . it was that bad.* This represented a complete dissolution of the relationship. The following year, a new president of the Center was elected in San Sisto, and the situation appeared completely changed for the women; the new president is reported to be showing support for them and interest in the Action Project, *our new president invited us officially.*

Individual attitudes and concerns shape what is identifiable as institutional action. In this case, the new president permitted women's involvement in decision making in the Center by inviting their attendance at the managing committee meeting. In the following sections, differences among women are shown, pointing out their varying influence in shaping institutional action. I analyze some transcripts taken from the videotapes of the managing committee meetings of the Senior Citizen Center of Monte Grillo and of San Sisto, in order to highlight the methods of communication used by the women, in particular Ida and Nina, in the actual course of the meetings. My focus is on the problems they encounter and the tactics they employ to face them.

THE WOMEN IN THE SENIOR CITIZEN CENTER OF MONTE GRILLO

In the Senior Citizen Center of Monte Grillo, a residential neighborhood of Perugia, there is a very active group of women who participate in the singing and theater worshops and in intergenerational activities in schools, all sponsored by the Action Project. Moreover, they contribute to the realization of initiatives promoted by the Senior Citizen Center itself, such as dinner parties, festivals, and so forth.

The next transcript is taken from a committee meeting of the Center at Monte Grillo immediately following a summer festival it organized. It was not an ordinary committee meeting, but was open to everyone who had contributed to the organization of the festival. It is significant to look at the seating arrangement during the meeting; the relevance of gender is immediately evident (see Fig. 5.1). The box represents the table where the

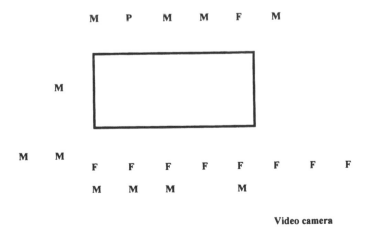

FIG. 5.1. Seating arrangement in an Action Project meeting at the Senior Citizen Center at Monte Grillo, showing male dominance. (M=Male; F=Female; P=President)

committee members are seated. Note that there is only one woman among them, Ida. The first row of chairs in front of the table is occupied entirely by women, facing the committee. The composition of the committee and the seating arrangement point to male dominance in the management of the Center. This is documented by both the organization of the turn taking and the content of the commitee members' verbal contributions.

WHO WORKS, WHO DECIDES

The festival was organized around voluntary work performed by the Center members. The main effort was put into organizing a canteen selling regional dishes as a form of fund raising. The women did the cooking. In the following exchange, the president is opening the meeting, thanking the women in particular for their contribution:

> **President:** well at this point I should say, first of all I should thank you all for what you have done because you rightly deserve all our thanks, our committee's thanks, because you really took a lot of trouble I imagine at the maximum of your effort all of you because without your contribution, we, men very probably could have done something but not much, and well we have to thank you openly because, your contribution has been enormous, (appreciating it) if we have to repeat it, that is to say that we we'll call you again we hope that you all will be ready as [now as this time to come therefore well,
>
> **Woman:**   [(   )
> **President:** to face the situation preferably not in three days because,
> **Woman:** [that's right
> **President:** [we realized that in three days, it was hard work and the results, [very good
> **Woman:** [(right right)
> **President:** from the organizational point of view and that of participation of course, but in relation, to financial matters it wasn't that successful, that is we didn't lose and we didn't gain
> (9/16/93 Open committee meeting of the Seniors Center of Monte Grillo)

Nina's comment, reported in a previous transcript (in chapter 1), *the men were always saying let's do this let's do that and we would run after them like sheep*, seems to fit the president's own comment. The president, in expressing his thanks to the women, constructs himself as the president, that is, the one properly delegated to do official thanking, *I should thank you all for what you have done because you rightly deserve all our thanks*; the institutional reference to "our" is made explicit, *our committee's thanks*.

The acknowledgment of the contribution of the women's work to the festival, *without your contribution, we, men very probably could have done something but not much*, is followed by an invitation to participate in future festivals, *we'll call you again we hope that you all will be ready as now*. Interestingly, the pro-term is switched from gender reference, *we, men*, to institutional reference, *we'll call you again*. There is an implication that the core of the institution is male, rather than female. Then the president announces the intention of extending the duration of the festival, which will imply a lengthening of hard work for the women, *to face the situation preferably not in three days*. It is interesting that the women express support, *that's right, right right*, and do not oppose the president's proposal.

Both from the seating arrangements and from just the opening remarks to the meeting, women appear to be cast as performers of decisions made exclusively by men. Women's initiatives are themselves actively resisted, as is pointed out through the analysis of the following transcripts.

WHAT SPACE FOR WOMEN'S INITIATIVES?

The following passage provides an instance of how resistance to woman's autonomous initiatives is conversationally produced in the course of the meeting at the Senior Citizen Center of Monte Grillo. Women's initiatives, conducted through the Action Project, are constructed as not belonging to the Center's initiatives, although the latter had officially agreed to participate in the Action Project. Also in this case, institutional conflicts seem to fade into gender conflicts.

Further on in the discussion, the president announces the Senior Center's activities program for the following year. One of the committee members is describing what was done the previous year at the Center and what the necessary changes in direction are, from his point of view:

Member: last year we started in February therefore we couldn't the election was in February

President: no in March

Member: no in March therefore we couldn't do much however since then we organized that party, we organized some dancing party et cetera but our program is not that, because we can't go on just organizing dancing parties we should seriously do something else then, all those activities, dance et cetera that though in my opinion they must be coordinated by the Center, in the most precise way, Ida speaks again about the theater workshop, of the

	theater as if it was something that comes from outside that is it is the Municipality that as Project et cetera et cetera asks us would you like to do the theater with us, participating in the Municipality's initiative let's do theater but why don't we take the initiative that is yes we yes do it do it as Center then if the Municipality likes what we do it'll take it, two, umm I believe that the relationship the relationship with school in the neighborhood is very important because we want to talk to the kids but we cannot give kids only, the soccer, on Sundays or something else it's not enough then to build up a bit of a relationship a bit of dialogue among older people. Generations of different of different
President:	categories
Member:	and kids, we have a a very easy way, you have just to be able to get in the school, I said that I had very beautiful experiences just a few days ago the president of the Senior Center of Panicale came to school and said I thank you for what you have done together with us last year
Tina:	we did something too [(with the theater)
Ida:	[we too
Member:	[yes but you did it not as Center though you did it individually, [( ) the school
Tina:	[( )
Member:	but I him ((indicating the President)) the Center didn't know anything about it if we organize a competition for um for the kids of the neighborhood a competition in which we say invent a symbol for Monte Grillo and then we say the best drawing will be awarded a prize of 300 thousands liras 500 400 thousands liras or a computer what you prefer you see the school is very receptive to these types of activities we have just to make a proposal but we have to make the proposal not him as Bianchi but us as the Center therefore she who knows things you who know things and you are able to tell them to kids, go to primary school but go there as Center
Woman:	not [(as an individual)
Member:	[not as an individual as an individual it doesn't matter,
Tina:	well
Member:	well then I want to say the program,
Women:	[( )
Member:	[the program is this that is the program we have to do is this (9/16/93 Open committee meeting of the Seniors Center of Monte Grillo)

This passage is intriguing, playing with ambiguities and conveying a sense of resistance to women's initiatives. The committee member speaking advocates the Senior Center's ownership of initiatives, *dance et cetera that though in my opinion they must be coordinated by the Center.* In particular, he objects to the theater workshop as an initiative not belonging to the Center, and Ida is made responsible for the intrusion, *Ida speaks again about the theater workshop, of the theater as if it was something that comes from outside.* Recall that it is mainly women who participate in this workshop run by a professional actress, who is paid by the Equal Opportunity Unit of the Municipality of Perugia, under the Action Project's budget.

This appears as an institutional conflict in defining respective fields of action. The theater workshop is constructed as being extraneous to the Center's activities, *it is the Municipality that as a Project asks us would you like to do the theater with us, participating in the Municipality's initiative.* (A similar conflict in defining institutional boundaries of action was pointed out by the president of the Senior Center of San Sisto [see p. 43].) The committee member proposes: *Why don't we take the initiative,* but what does this mean? Is the Center prepared to run the workshop autonomously and pay the professional? Or does the Center intend to determine the contents of the activity? *Do it as Center then if the Municipality likes what we do it'll take it.* Answers to these questions are not forthcoming. In any case, this member is objecting to the theater workshop because it is part of the Action Project, belonging to a different institution. This is an open contradiction with the fact that the Center at Monte Grillo officially agreed to take part in the Action Project. Therefore, the theater initiatives should have been considered integral to the Center's work.

Initiatives in the schools are then presented as a relevant field of action for the Senior Center, *the relationship with the school in the neighborhood is very important.* Tina's claim, *we did something too,* is interrupted (Makri-Tsilipakou, 1994; Murata, 1994; West & Zimmerman, 1985) by the committee member's objection, *but you did it not as Center though you did it individually.* In this case, the women's initiative is disqualified as not representative of the Center, because it was carried out on an individual basis, *but I him ((indicating the President)) the Center didn't know anything about it.*

One of the main emphases of the Older Women's Action Project has been to promote bonding activities between generations in local schools. The initiatives that Tina refers to are thus an integral part of the Project, although none of the women makes this explicit. Is this a problem of bad communication between members and the managing committee? This member again objects to the women's initiative, defining their action as unrelated to the Senior Citizen Center. He could have asked for information about such activities, and could have begun including them in the program of the Center. He instead objects to their belonging to the Center, thus creating resistance. On the one hand, women cannot propose initiatives developed in a different institution than the Center, that is, the Equal Opportunity Unit; on the other hand, supposedly individual women's initiatives are disqualified. This is a bind that implies that no space exists for women's initiatives. Here, as was noted earlier (see p. 46), the resistance to a different institutional influence fades into resistance to women's autonomous initiative.

Foucault (1982), in describing power relationships, pointed out:

> In itself the exercise of power is not violence; nor is it a consent which, implicitly, is renewable. It is a total structure of actions brought to bear upon possible actions; it incites, it induces, it seduces, it makes easier or more difficult; in the extreme it constrains or forbids absolutely; it is nevertheless always a way of acting upon an acting subject or acting subjects by virtue of their acting or being capable of action. A set of actions upon other actions. (p. 220)

From this perspective, women must be maintained as "acting subjects," active members who participate in initiatives of the Center; only their taking the initiative themselves must be contained.

My intention is now to point out that what is occurring in Monte Grillo is due in part to the men's resistance, but also to the women's lack of communication skills. A very different situation is observable at the Center of San Sisto, where women are more supported, and one of them in particular is a good communicator. My theoretical interest here is to show how idiosyncratic personal differences influence social processes. This can significantly contribute to an understanding of how the social construction of identity is interrelated with the production of institutional contexts. Not only do institutional discourses and practices influence identity production, but social identities and idiosyncratic personal characteristics influence the production of social contexts.

Near the end of the committee meeting, a woman is soliciting Ida to present the Action Project initiatives for the following year. She is apparently concerned that the women will be overextended in thier activities:

Carla:	Listen just listen to me Ida excuse me but you didn't say anything about the Women's Project if we do this we cannot do the other
Ida:	for?
Woman:	for the Women's Project
Ida:	well [for the Women's Project we have a conference
Woman:	[( )
Carla:	and how could we manage to do one and [the other

Ida: [we have this in November
Woman: [(   )
         ((the President looks down with his arms crossed))
Tina: no. Now we have this international conference
Ida: eh!
Tina: [of the Women's Project
Member: [no I say what you do (   ) the women will do it as the Center
Woman: we have to do it as the Center
Ida: but it does correspond to the Center too, doesn't it? ((turning
         towards the camera)) as Center too all together doing it in this
         way but how,
Tina: in fact if the lady is here in fact if the lady is here is just
Ida: for this
Tina: to see what happens in the Centers
         (9/16/93 Open committee meeting of the Seniors Center of
         Monte Grillo)

Carla asks Ida, the only woman on the committee, to present the Action
Project initiatives, *but you didn't say anything about the Women's Project,* for
practical reasons, *if we do this we cannot do the other.* This brief passage is
particularly enlightening because it shows the women's—specifically Ida
and Tina's—lack of skill in effectively communicating the content of the
initiatives decided by the committee for which they are delegates to members of the meeting. They announce, *for the Women's Project we have a
conference,* without adding any further explanation regarding the aim,
content, and modality of participation of the international meeting. Also
shown is male resistance: No interest or request for an explanation is raised
by the president or the other committee members, *((the President looks down
with his arms crossed))*, but there is further objection on the ownership of the
activities that cuts off Tina's turn, *I say what you do . . . do it as Center we
have to do it as Center.* In this case the committee member opens up a
possibility of including of the Action Project in the Center's initiatives. Ida
immediately picks up on this offer, highlighting the convergence between
the Center's and the Action Project's activities, *but it does correspond as
Center too.* The researcher's presence is used as a proof, *in fact if the lady is
here . . . is just . . . to see what happens in the Centers.*

Recall Rita's self-reprimand, *we had to clarify well,* that turned into
complaint, *they don't listen to us* (p. 48); what Rita described is happening in
this transcript. Certainly the women do not pose their points strongly; but
they are also ignored by the committee: Nobody asks for explanations or
expresses interest. Ida's lack of communication skill contributes to the
difficulties in introducing the Action Project activities, produced by a

climate of resistance toward women's autonomous initiatives. A more positive situation is observable at the Center in San Sisto, examined next.

THE NEW PRESIDENT OF THE
SENIOR CITIZEN CENTER OF SAN SISTO

The Senior Citizen Center of San Sisto was the first one to have been established in the Municipality of Perugia in 1986. The available space, consisting of many rooms dispersed across three floors, allows for the conduct of different activities simultaneously. Playing cards is a popular entertainment here, along with exercise classes, woodwork, and sewing workshops, as well as the singing and theater workshops connected to the Action Project.

Since the election of the new president, the situation for the women underwent a radical change. As Nina reported (see p. 61), the new president of the Center in San Sisto was favorably disposed to the Action Project and had invited the women to take part in the managing committee. Examining some transcripts from a videotape of a meeting, I can report that a certain level of resistance toward the women is conveyed by committee members, but it is met effectively and forcefully by Nina's responses.

It is important to point out that, although a more positive situation for the women can be observed in this Center, women are still assigned traditional female tasks, like cooking: More than one third of the meeting is devoted to the discussion of the menu for a forthcoming dinner party, organized by the Center, and such matters are clearly constructed as women's concerns. This is noticeable, for example, in the interventions of two male members of the committee: *Since the ladies are here it's the case to decide the menu; let's leave the decision to women (on this topic) ee the women's kingdom is the kitchen.*

The following transcripts illustrate several of Nina's attempts to introduce information about the Action Project activities into the meeting. The discussion is now focused on the program of activities for the next year. The celebration of "women's day" has just been introduced:

President: then there's the eighth of March=
Nina: =women's day after after I must [also say something on this,
President: [yes yes, all right ((taking agenda out of a pocket))
Nina: [(on this)
President: [the eighth of March. Let's just see what day is it. March the fifth is Saturday
Lino: the fifth is Saturday

President: the eighth is [Tuesday [Tuesday is the eighth
Woman: [Tuesday
Nina: [Tuesday, very well
President: we do it the day, [the day of the festivity ((looking at Nina))
Nina: [yes yes the same day [in all the Centers (   )
President: [what, well what shall
            we do
Nina: but I'd say=
President: =a conference as in past years? ((again looking at Nina)) (   )
Nina: [but
Vera: [yes who did come last year she was coming   [the
President: [the one or the
            other
Lino: the Giannetta,
Vera: no
Lino: [that one
President: [(the Giannetta came [few times)
Vera: [that one from (Terni)
Nina: shall we do that work that they did at the Penna building?
President: that'd be nice
Nina: eh? (then) I'll inform Tonia Neri and we try to do it here too it
            would be nice that one eh, ((president nods)) with the slides and
            everything, a work (   ), really for women I think [it is a work
President: [we may in-
            vite the Councillor [who tells us ten word and if she makes it too
            long we cut her tongue ((smiling))
Nina: [yes yes yes eh yes of course of course
            (2/19/94 Managing committee meeting of the Senior Citizen
            Center of San Sisto)

When the president introduces the topic, *eighth of March*, Nina jumps in
and tells the group her desire to communicate some news on the subject,
=women's day after . . . I must also say something on this. The president,
assenting, speaks over Nina, *yes yes, all right*, and carries on with what he
was doing, *((taking agenda out of a pocket))*.

In this exchange, the women's day is constructed by the president as
Nina's concern, and Nina collaborates in this construction. In having to
decide when to hold the celebration, *we do it the day . . . of the festivity*, the
president turns towards Nina, *((looking at Nina))*, who promptly replies, *yes
yes the same day, in all the Centers*. Moreover, for the choice of the activity,
what, well what shall we do, Nina is the first one to attempt a reply, *but I'd
say=*, even though there are four other women in the meeting. The
president finishes Nina's sentence making a proposal of his own, *=a*

conference as in past years?, continuing to give Nina status as privileged interlocutor, *((again looking at Nina)).*

A brief discussion as to whom to invite follows, but it is glossed by the president as irrelevant, *one or the other.* Nina proposes a completely new thing: a slide show, *shall we do that work that they did at the Penna building?,* describing the product of a photography workshop on reminiscence using old personal photos, carried out by the women under the auspices of the Action Project. Nina not only is able to bring an Action Project product into the context of her Center, but she is also very effective in introducing the proposal into the flow of the conversation.

As the president has given his assent, *that'd be nice,* Nina assumes the responsibility for organizing the show, volunteering to contact the workshop organizer, *I'll inform Tonia Neri and we try to do it here too,* describing it as particularly appropriate for the occasion, *a work (   ), really for women I think.* She is interrupted by the president, who proposes to invite a councillor to the show, *we may invite the councillor.*

In the next transcript, Nina again shows her effective communication skills. The committee is now discussing the program of trips for the year, with the overlapping of different events being the issue at hand:

President:	now we have to decide the trips that we want to do
Tino:	well, [I decided,
President:	[that's it, let's see
Tino:	no decided I made a program, but this program, until March, is over because the eighth of March there's women's day, the
Nina:	the 13th
Tino:	the 13th the social dinner
Nina:	no no the [19th
Vera:	[the 19th
Nina:	excuse me since we are talking about women's day I'd like to do this little report that is part of Women's Project
President:	yes yes
Tino:	when is the social dinner isn't there the social dinner
President:	on the 19th
	. . .
Tino:	the 19th was that one of the election, [and the 13th of March
President:	[on the 19th of March assembly and election
Lino:	OK
President:	the 13th what is it
Tino:	the 13th of March I think I might be wrong I eh I think that we have the social dinner, in preparation also for the election of the 19th=

> Nina: =I'll take the turn ((raising her hand)) this is not absolutely because on the 13th I was already engaged, with the Action Project, because we have Women's day on the 13th of March (2/18/94 Managing committee meeting of the Senior Citizen Center of San Sisto)

The member who has prepared a program for the trips signals problems in the timing of the trips because of other events, *this program, until March, is over.* Hearing Lino mention women's day, Nina intervenes, introducing again her intention to report some news on the subject, *since we are talking about women's day I'd like to do this little report that is part of Women's Project.* The president assents, *yes yes,* yet carries on with the business at hand: overlapping dates, interacting with Tino, *when is the social dinner.*

In the course of the discussion about the dates, Nina intervenes forcefully, =*I'll take the turn ((raising her hand)) this is not absolutely,* and she prevents the possibility of an overlap between the Action Project Women's Day celebration and some other Center activities, *on the 13th I was already engaged, with the Action Project, because we have women's day on the 13th of March.*

Halfway through the meeting, for the third time, Nina introduces her intention to communicate news to the group and, this time, she manages to read her report from the last committee meeting of the Action Project. The discussion is focused on solidarity activities. Nina announces that she has something to say about it, and then starts presenting her report. This passage represents a quite unusual transcript, insofar as it illustrates the reading aloud of a written report; but it is significant in giving an idea of Nina's ability to successfully inform:

> Nina: Then now I tell you
> President: ( )
> Nina: here here there is already, in this report that I'll do on what we did, on the seventh, on the seventh of February ((taking a block note)) what was said, in our meeting (that was) for one thing, Ellera Corciano and the Alessandro Volta in Terni joined the Action Project, therefore they were they participated them too well they participate in the Action Project, then we talked about solidarity, and about the trip we have to do to London and women's day so ((reading)) about solidarity after various ideas it seems that the most feasible would be to create a group of people who participate in this initiative, and through a person already introduced because there must be somebody who who knows how, [( ) to develop the thing

Vera: [to develop this thing, of course
Nina: ((turning page)) (just) in that environment well then of solidarity
             to send these volunteers where there is greater need of their help,
             therefore, it'll be a telephone line
             . . .

Nina: ((starting again to read)) then it was for the trip to London that
             was in the program there is a trip to London, a theater group
             isgoing to perform there, they choose some people (   ) and who
             work for a longer time in the Action Project, after having
             evaluated for a while emm and discussed we came to this con-
             clusion, and the names of the women who were present were
             called out at the last theater workshop that was held, for women's
             day then there'd be a party very likely here at the Sodalizio di San
             Martino, we said on the 21st but some Centers had trips, and
             other meetings therefore we decided for the 13th.
President: of March
Nina: 13th of March that's it this there'll be a meeting the lunch there
             at the Sodalizio di San Martino and then there'll be a fashion
             parade in the afternoon with a dancing party, this then for the
             price that we'll pay as usual it'll be the lunch and something more
             to pay the band well this is still to be decided the prize, that's it,
             this was said then we should meet, to decide, other points, that's
             it
Ivo: ([   )
Vera: [excuse me Nina
Ivo: that we attach it to the minutes [(   )
Nina: [yes yes no problem yes yes I do
             it for you and I take it to you
             (2/19/94 Managing committee meeting of the Senior Citizen
             Center of San Sisto)

Having a written report allows Nina to inform the committee exhaustively on all the main events, *Ellera Corciano and the Alessandro Volta in Terni
joined the Action Project*, and future initiatives, *about solidarity . . . to create a
group of people; a trip to London, a theater group is going to perform there; 13th
of March that's it this there'll be a meeting the lunch there at the Sodalizio di San
Martino and then there'll be a fashion parade in the afternoon with a dancing
party*, of the Action Project. Moreover, the committee member, who is
writing the minutes of the meeting, asks Nina to include her report, *we attach
it to the minutes*, in so doing the report contents become officially recognized
as part of what was said at the meeting.

The transcripts analyzed in the two preceding sections show consistent
differences in Ida's and Nina's conversational skills and in their abilities to

sustain their point of view, as well as different levels of resistance toward women's initiatives being conveyed. Nina's effective communication skills allow her to introduce women's initiatives into the activities of the Center of San Sisto, whereas in Monte Grillo, women's initiatives are constructed as extraneous to the Center and space is not available to women to develop autonomous activities. Both women's and committee members' personal attitudes and skills contribute to shaping identifiable institutional activities.

TWO DIFFERENT OUTCOMES

The difficulties that Ida met in her Center, as just documented, can partially account for a "curious" proposal she made in the course of one of the last committee meetings of the Action Project. The meeting was mainly focused on the topic of the creation of the European Older Women's Network. Ida suggested including men in the network, causing a heated and lengthy discussion. Only the first part of it is reproduced here:

Ida:	in my opinion thiiis um network I said, couldn't we also involve men in it could we, doesn't, this idea go
Elia:	excuse me
Woman:	see you later
Ida:	bye Elia
Elia:	we'll meet down there [( )
Nina:	[the men (you want to involve)
Ida:	with men too a bit the men too isn't that so? no we will always keep being [((an up/down movement with her hands)) no always
Nina:	[and no but then ( )
	((some women are talking together))
Ida:	to keep always us ((front/back movement with her left hand)) but well, wouldn't it be good to give us a hand because they have their ideas too to give to us I don't know what do you think
Nina:	we have lots of ideas that we could sell to them and not they [(to us)
Ida:	[well perhaps something more according to the points of view now
Officer:	now answer [this question,
Ida:	[(answer)
Officer:	I think it is a basic one we could even finish here
Ida:	[and you what do you say
Alma:	[listen listen Ida [the men, many of them (my dear) come away but

```
     Lola:                        [(   )
       Ida:    [yes yes but
     Alma:    [(   ) I am the master but [my wife is the boss
       Ida:                              [listen not all, not all would be the
              same isn't it so? there must be one also some who can be
              [(   )
   Woman:    [there is (   )
     Alma:    yes yes
     Delia:   ( some modern ones there are )
     Nina:    listen one thing in our Center, there are always men we arrived
              to have nine nine women, in the committee, there are nine of
              them,
     Nilla:   [(   )
     Nina:    [well before we were not in the committee but we had to go
              anyway even if we were not in the committee
     Nilla:   [they would call us because there were no men
     Nina:    [because, because they want the women it's useless to involve
              men and then we have to work we are the ones who work
              (3/25/94 Committee meeting of the Action Project)
```

Couldn't we also involve men in it, is a bolt out of the blue. The very construction of this sentence expresses hesitation, with two pauses and a restart: *could we, doesn't, this idea go.* Ida's turn is followed by silence, filled in by Elia's departure and goodbyes. Then Nina replies with an ironic inflection, *the men (you want to involve).* Ida explains her idea through gestures, more than through what she says: The hand movements, *((an up/down movement with her hands)), ((front/back movement with her left hand))*, represent the centrality of women in the network; then she repeats her idea of including men, *they have their ideas too to give to us.* Nina sharply replies, directly contrasting Ida's proposal, *we have lots of ideas that we could sell to them and not they (to us).*

The officer signals the relevance of Ida's proposal for the future of the network, *I think it is a basic one we could even finish here*, but she declines to answer Ida's question herself, delegating this to the group, *now answer this question.* Nina expands on her initial reply, announcing proudly, *we arrived to have nine nine women, in the committee, there are nine of them.* The motivation for her opposition to men's participation is made explicit by referring to women's active role in the life of the Center, in comparison to that of the men, *it's useless to involve men and then we have to work we are the ones who work.*

The Action Project has produced a space for women's initiatives and leadership that has different implications at the personal and institutional levels. Nina, being outspoken and organized, has managed to have the

Action Project initiatives successfully integrated into the Center. This occurred with the support of her president. Once women of the Senior Center of San Sisto recognized their active role in the life of the Center, they started to want, and then obtained, participation in the decision-making process. In this case, the composition of the Senior Center's managing committee changed.

For Ida, it is a completely different matter. Apparently, she has been finding it difficult to face the resistance she meets in the Center of Monte Grillo. To propose the inclusion of men in the Older Women's Network can be interpreted as an attempt to minimize the gender division that she rightly sees as the source of male resistance encountered at her Center. Her proposal might have consequences for the institution of the Network.

The interplay of personal motives and institutional agendas is rather complex and interactive in nature. Nina is allowed to be more influential because of a more supportive environment, but probably also due to her forceful manner. In contrast, the strong resistance met by Ida contributes to shrinking her already limited communication skills.

There is a complex interrelationship that must be understood in context. In fact, recall that Nina's effective communication skills were not sufficient to guarantee her Center participation in the Action Project when dealing with the previous president. In the analysis of the transcripts presented in this chapter, different personal identities are projected for Nina and Ida, and they appear to influence, and to be influenced by, the social and institutional setting of the action.

6

Conclusion:
Understanding Social Change

Studying the social production of identity has allowed me to look at the intricate intermingling of the personal, social, and institutional dimensions of everyday reality. This topic, more than others, is useful in exploring the complexity of the process of social change as well as the process of social reproduction and maintenance, whether at a personal, social, or institutional level.

Membership categories have been shown to be at the core of identity work. The stability of the categories, as shared social knowledge, contrasts with the variability of their actual use. In fact, a sense of idiosyncratic personal identity is achieved by members through both contrast and association with different membership categories. Categories are used as a background upon which specific personal relevancies may emerge. It appears that the stability of membership categories is compensated for by a high level of variability in their actual conversational use and therefore in the local management of specific personal identities. This study has shown various examples of women distancing and rejecting membership in the category "old" and its negative connotation.

Conforming to typified social knowledge as well as distancing from it are both available alternatives to members. What "being old" means is not something defined or definable once and for all, but it is constantly negotiated in the actual occurrence of concrete circumstances.

From this perspective, ageism, sexism, and racism can be seen as forms and degrees of adherence to social typifications, that is to membership categories, in relation to specific members' activities and discourses. What I have attempted to show here is how the use of categories is bound to specific settings and occasions. Also, such use is motivated by specific events and the interactional developments within each event. It is not something decided once and for all, in individual heads. It is contextual and interactional.

Social reproduction and/or change appear to be produced by members' constant negotiation of actual circumstances. In this regard, marginalization

78

of the elderly cannot be fought through generalized actions. First, processes of marginalization and exclusion should be studied by exploring the concrete circumstances in which specific members decide to endorse social typifications, in relation to definite social and institutional settings. Then, it would be necessary to find the effective actions to be employed to stop marginalization in relation to those specific practices.

Institutional intervention has been pointed out as a catalyst to either social change or social reproduction. Some institutions have a positive mobilizing effect on women's gender and age identification processes, others have a negative and limiting effect. In particular, I have shown how older women can experience new and exciting activities through institutional intervention, and that mobilize a new sense of identity.

The Action Project opened spaces for women's initiatives; at the same time, however, those efforts were resisted in some of the Senior Citizen Centers, through a complex interplay of personal and institutional influences, in which members' personal identities had an important impact. In fact, it has been pointed out how different women's communication skills, aims and perspective could more or less mediate Action Project initiatives in the Senior Citizen Centers. Some women were more successful than others in this respect. Moreover, women's initiatives encountered various degrees of resistance and/or support in relation to different institutional subjects.

A further problematic aspect of institutional influence on identity processes was pointed out, that is, how institutional priorities and procedures (institutional accountability, institutions' organizational procedures, institutional conflicts) are made present and meaningful and how they affect women, by the action and discourses of institutional subjects. The influence of specific institutions—that is, institutional activities, procedures, and objectives—on identity production processes is, therefore, complex.

Further studies should explore in particular how institutional needs, such as personnel shifts or specific routines, impinge on identity production among the elderly. Given the devastating psychological effects that are often visible upon entry into nursing homes and hospitals, the approach to identity construction used in this book should be applied to those other institutions.

Awareness of the processes of identity production of elderly people would undoubtedly be very useful in the training of personnel working with them, showing in detail the effects of ordinary institutional practices in hospitals, nursing homes, and senior centers on identity processes. The commonsense discourses and practices related to elderliness must also be taught, as, for example, the typifications discussed in this book.

Features of gender identity have been pointed out as well. Feminine identity seemed to be bound to moral duties relating to caregiving restrictions and limitations in the sphere of personal action, as well as diminished visibility and exclusion from decision making. Women in this study were bound in several ways to the home sphere and were given limited access to public spaces.

The great occurrence of mobility problems and psychological disorders among older women could be connected to such home confinement. Older women's morbidity should be studied in relation to social and institutional practices related to femininity, in particular in relation to women's restricted spheres of action. Epidemiological trends could have a basis not only in biological differences but in gender-specific practices that create a specific vulnerability to certain illness.

Gender identity was explored in particular in relation to institutional interventions. Several instances of conflicts among institutional participants over either restricting or broadening women's initiative were discussed. Equal-opportunity legislation was used by institutional subjects as a resource in their talk to sustain the relevance and value of promoting women's leadership and autonomy. Thus, the salience of the larger political and societal context in shaping members' identity work is quite visible in this study.

"Being old" appears to be a very different condition for men and women. Such differences should be taken into account in planning services for elderly people, especially considering the substantial majority of women among older people. It appears clear from this study that creating a Senior Citizen Center is not sufficient to guarantee equal use or access to services by both men and women. It is also no guarantee that women, although active members, will be permitted to take part in the decision making at the Center.

Through the analysis of concrete instances of interactions, the concept of identity appeared in all its kaleidescopic character, ever-changing and somewhat elusive. If, from a theoretical point of view, there was a risk of the dissolution of the subject, on an empirical level the creativity of the subject was mainly highlighted. It is the subject's sense-making, the constant interpretive work conducted by members in carrying out their ordinary activities, that holds together, produces, and reproduces the stable features of social and institutional settings, as well as members' identities. It is here that each subject's identity resides and here that no dissolution is possible.

Practical reasoning is essentially generative in character; it is productive of concrete circumstances, which lead such reasoning toward definite outcomes. From this perspective, we can start to understand the power that constructions of elderliness have in shaping our own aging process, in flesh and blood: Isolation, decrement, and despair are one possibility; integration, health, and well-being are the other.

Appendix A:
Transcript Notations

Transcript notations are developed from M. J. Atkinson and Heritage (1984). They are kept to a minimum to increase readability. Transcribing is already a form of theorizing (Baker, 1990; Ochs, 1979); in the case of videotapes, the transcription cannot be carried out without a definite interpretative hypothesis, such as its richness (Lukas, 1987). In a few instances, I went back to the video data while analyzing the transcripts, because missing details or incoherence were noticeable. Moreover, the translation from Italian to English implies further mediations relating to the video data (Moerman, 1996). Ambiguity or incoherence in the transcripts, common in spoken language, had to be resolved in the translation; therefore, I always carried out the analysis using the original transcripts in Italian. Where the meaning of an entire sentence or phrase could not be attained, the English is a direct translation of the Italian words.

. or ,	Stop or pause in the rhythm of the conversation
?	Rising intonation
!	Excited tone
( )	word(s) spoken, but not audible
(dog)	word(s) whose hearing is doubtful
((laugh))	Transcriber description
[	overlapping utterances at this point
=	no gaps in the flow of conversation

Appendix B:
List of the Data Collected

All of the events were video-recorded, apart from the first meeting, which was audiotaped.

9/10/92	Committee meeting of the Action Project
10/ 9/92	Committee meeting of the Action Project
11/13/92	Committee meeting of the Action Project
12/18/92	Committee meeting of the Action Project
1/15/93	Committee meeting of the Action Project
1/25/93	Theater workshop at Montegrillo
	Theater workshop at Ponte San Giovanni
2/ 5/93	Committee meeting of the Action Project
3/ 9/93	Committee meeting of the Action Project
4/19/93	Managing committee meeting of the Senior Center of Ponte Felcino
5/10/93	Committee meeting of the Action Project
5/31/93	Committee meeting of the Action Project
9/15/93	Committee meeting of the Action Project
9/16/93	Managing committee meeting of the Senior Center of Monte Grillo
12/10/93	Committee meeting of the Action Project
2/ 8/94	Committee meeting of the Action Project
2/19/94	Managing committee meeting of the Senior Center of San Sisto
2/22/94	Committee meeting of the Action Project
3/ ?/94	Theater workshop at San Sisto
3/25/94	Committee meeting of the Action Project
5/ 2/94	Committee meeting of the Action Project

References

Adelman, R. D., Greene, M. G., Charon, R., & Friedmann, E. (1992). The content of physician and elderly patient interaction in the medical primary care encounter. *Communication Research, 19*(3), 370–380.

Ainlay, S. C., & Redfoot, D. L. (1982). Ageing and identity-in-the-word: A phenomenological analysis. *International Journal of Ageing and Human Development, 15*(1), 1–16.

Arber, S., & Ginn, J. (1991). *Gender and later life.* London: Sage.

Atkinson, M. A., Cuff, E. C., & Lee, J. R. (1978). The recommencement of a meeting as a member's accomplishment. In J. Schenkein (Ed.), *Studies in the organization of conversational interaction* (pp. 57–77). New York: Academic Press.

Atkinson, M. J. (1984). Public speaking and audience responses: Some techniques for inviting applause. In M. J. Atkinson & J. Heritage (Eds.), *Structures of social action: Studies in conversational analysis.* Cambridge, UK: Cambridge University Press.

Atkinson, M. J., & Heritage, J. (Eds.). (1984). *Structures of social action: Studies in conversational analysis.* Cambridge, UK: Cambridge University Press.

Atkinson, P. (1985). Talk and identity: Some convergences in micro-sociology. In H. J. Helle & S. N. Eisenstadt (Eds.), *Micro-sociological theory* (Vol. 2, pp. 117–132). London: Sage.

Baker, C. (1983). A "second look" at interviews with adolescents. *Journal of Youth and Adolescence, 12*(6), 501–519.

Baker, C. (1984). The "search for adultness": Membership work in adolescent–adult talk. *Human Studies, 7,* 301–323.

Baker, C. (1990). *Transcriptions: Characterising classrooms and speakers.* Unpublished paper presented at the 15th Australian Reading Association Conference, Canberra.

Baker, C., & Keogh, J. (1995). *Accounting for achievement in parent–teacher interviews.* Human Studies, 18(2/3), 263–300.

Baltes, M. M., & Carstensen, L. L. (1996). The process of successful ageing, *Ageing and Society, 16,* 397–422.

Barbato, C. A., & Perse, E. M. (1992). Interpersonal communication motives and the life position of elders. *Communication Research, 19*(4), 516–531.

Barer, B. M. (1994). Men and women aging differently. *International Journal of Aging and Human Development, 38*(1), 24–90.

Beckingham, A. C., & Watt, S. (1995). daring to grow old: Lessons in healthy aging and empowerment. *Educational Gerontology, 21,* 479–495.

Bengtson, V. L. (1973). Aging and the social system. In V. L. Bengtson (Ed.), *The social psychology of aging* (pp. 15–31). New York: Bobbs-Merrill.

Bilmes, J. (1992). Mishearings. In G. Watson & R. M. Seiler (Ed.), *Text in context* (pp. 79–98). Newbury Park, CA: Sage.

Boden, D. (1994). *The business of talk.* Cambridge, MA: Polity.

Boden, D., & Bielby, D. (1983). The past as a resouce: A conversational analysis of elderly talk. *Human Development, 26*, 308–319.

Boden, D., & Bielby, D. (1986). The way it was: Topical organization in elderly conversation. *Language and Communication, 6*(1/2), 73–89.

Bultena, G. L., & Powers, E. A. (1978). Denial of ageing: Age identification and reference group orientation. *Journal of Gerontology, 33*, 748–754.

Caporael, L. (1981). The paralanguage of caregiving: Baby talk to the institutionalized aged. *Journal of Personality and Social Psychology, 40*(5), 876–884.

Caporael, L., & Culbertson, G. H. (1983). Baby talk speech to the elderly: Complexity and content of message. *Personality and Social Psychology Bulletin, 9*(2), 305–312.

Caporael, L., & Culbertson, G. H. (1986). Verbal response modes of baby-talk and other speech at institutions for the aged. *Language and Communication, 6*(1/2), 99–112.

Carver, C. S., & de la Garza, N. H. (1984). Schema-guided information search in stereotyping of the elderly. *Journal of Applied Social Psychology, 14*(1), 69–81.

Cohen, G., & Faulkner, D. (1986). Does "elder's speak" work? The effect of intonation and stress on comprehension and recall of spoken discourse in old age. *Language and Communication, 6*(1/2), 91–98.

Cooper, M., & Sydell, M. (Eds.). (1994). *Lewisham older women's health survey.* London: EdRop The City Lit.

Coopmans, M., Harrop, A., & Hermans-Huiskes, M. (1988). *The social and economic situation of older women in Europe* (Joint Report of Two Research Projects). Commission of the European Communities, Directorate-General Employment, Social Affairs, and Education, Brussels.

Coupland, J., & Coupland, N. (1994). "Old age doesn't come alone": Discursive representations of health-in-aging in geriatric medicine. *International Journal of Aging and Human Development, 39*(1), 81–95.

Coupland, N., & Coupland, J. (1989). Age identity and elderly disclosure of chronological age. *York Papers in Linguistics, 13*, 77–88.

Coupland, N., & Coupland, J. (1990). Language in later life. In H. Giles & W. P. Robinson (Eds.), *Handbook of Language and Social Psychology* (pp. 451–468). Chichester: Wiley.

Coupland, N., Coupland, J., & Giles, H. (1989). Telling age in later life: Identity and face implications. *Text, 9*(2), 129–151.

Coupland, N., Coupland, J., & Giles, H. (1991). *Language, society and the elderly.* Cambridge, MA: Blackwell.

Coupland, N., Coupland, J., Giles, H., & Henwood, K. (1988). Accommodating the elderly: Invoking and extending a theory, *Language in Society, 17*, 1–41.

Coupland, N., Coupland, J., Giles, H., & Henwood, K. (1991). Formulating age: Dimensions of age identity in elderly talk. *Discourse Processes, 14*, 87–106.

Coupland, N., Coupland, J., Giles, H., Henwood, K., & Wiemann, J. (1988). Elderly self-disclosure: Interactional and intergroup issues. *Language and Communication, 8*(2), 109–133.

Coupland, N., Coupland, J., & Grainger, K. (1991). Intergenerational discourse: Contextual versions of ageing and elderliness. *Ageing and Society, 11*, 189–208.

Cuff, E. C., & Payne, G. C. F. (Eds.), (1979). *Perspectives in sociology.* London: George Allen & Unwin.

Cuff, E. C., & Sharrock, W. W. (1985). Meetings. In T. A. van Dijk (Ed.), *Handbook of discourse analysis* (Vol. 3, pp. 149–159). London: Academic Press.

Dreher, B. B. (1987). *Communication skills for working with elders.* New York: Springer.

Duranti, A., & Goodwin, C. (1992). *Rethinking context.* Cambridge, UK: Cambridge University Press.

Facchini, C., & Scortegagna, R. (1993). Italia: Alternative all'istituzionalizzazione e ruolo centrale delle donne [Italy: Alternatives to institutionalization and the women's central role]. In F. Lesemann & C. Martin (Eds.), *Assistenza a domicilio famiglia e anziani* [Home care family and elderly] (pp. 33–109). Milano: Angeli.

Foucault, M. (1978). *The history of sexuality: Vol. 1. An introduction.* New York: Pantheon Books.

Foucault, M. (1982). The subject and power. In H. Dreyfus & P. Robinow (Eds.), *Michael Foucault: Beyond structuralism and hermeneutics* (pp. 208–226). Brighton, Sussex, England: The Harvester Press.

Garfinkel, H. (1967). *Studies in ethnomethodology.* Englewood Cliffs, NJ: Prentice-Hall.

Gergen, K. J., & Davis, K. E. (1985). *The social construction of the person.* New York: Springer-Verlag.

Gergen, K. J., & Gergen, M. M. (1983). Narratives of the self. In T. R. Sarbin & K. E. Scheibe (Eds.), *Studies in social identity* (pp. 254–273). New York: Praeger.

Gilleard, C. (1996). Consumption and identity in later life: Toward a cultural gerontology. *Ageing and Society, 16,* 489–498.

Ginn, J. (1992). *Grey power, gender and class.* Paper presented at the Critical Social Policy Conference, University of North London, London, UK.

Ginn, J., & Arber, S. (1991). Gender, class and income inequalities in later life. *British Journal of Sociology, 42*(3), 367–396.

Ginn, J., & Arber, S. (1992). Towards women's independence: Pension system in three contrasting european welfare states. *Journal of European Social Policy, 4*(2), 255–277.

Green, B. S. (1993). *Gerontology and the construction of old age.* New York: De Gruyter.

Harold, S. (1992). Education in later life: The case of older women. *Educational Gerontology, 18*(5), 511–527.

Hepworth, M. (1996). "William" and the old folks: Notes on infantilisation. *Ageing and Society, 16,* 423–441.

Heritage, J. (1984). *Garfinkel and ethnomethodology.* Cambridge, UK: Polity.

Hermanova, H. (1995). Healthy aging in Europe in the 1990s and implications for education and training in the care of the elderly. *Educational Gerontology, 21,* 1–14.

Jayyusi, L. (1984). *Categorization and the moral order.* London: Routledge & Kegan Paul.

Kamler, B. (1995). *From autobiography to collective biography: Writing workshop practices with women 60–80.* Paper presented at the annual meeting of the America Educational Research Association, San Francisco.

Kamler, B., & Feldman, S. (1996). Mirror mirror on the wall: Reflection on ageing. *Australian Cultural History, 14,* 1–22.

Laws, G. (1995). Understanding ageism: Lessons from feminism and postmodernism. *The Gerontologist, 35*(1), 112–118.

Levin, J., & Levin, W. C. (1980). *Ageism: Prejudice and discrimination against the elderly.* Belmont, CA: Wadsworth.

Lomax, P. (Ed.). (1989). *The managment of change.* Clevedon: Multilingual Matters Ltd.

Lukas, W. (1987). *The thematic analysis of videotaped interaction.* Unpublished manuscript, University of Surrey, Guildford, England.

Macellari, L. (1981). La produzione sociale della personalità dell'anziano [The social production of the elder's personality]. In Gli anziani in Umbria, *Quaderni della Regione dell'Umbria, 3*(1), 114, 49–70.

Makri-Tsilipakou, M. (1994). Interruption revisited: Affiliative vs. disaffiliative intervention. *Journal of Pragmatics, 21*(4), 401–426.

McNiff, J. (1988). *Action research: Principles and practice.* London: Collier McMillan.

Mengani, M., & Gagliardi, C. (1993). *Older women in the European Community: Social and economic conditions.* Italian Report, INRCA, Ancona, Italy.

Mengani, M., & Lamura, G. (1995). Elderly women, family structure and care patterns in Italy. In G. Dooghe & N. Appleton (Eds.), *Elderly women in Europe* (pp. 121–141). Bruxelles: Centrum vor Bevolkings.

Moen, P., Dempster-McClain, D., & Williams, R. M. (1992). Successful aging: A life-course perspective on women's multiple roles and health. *American Journal of Sociology, 97*(6), 1612–1638.

Moerman, M. (1996). The field of analysing foreign language conversations. *Journal of Pragmatics, 26,* 147–158.

Montepare, J. M., & Lachman, M. E. (1989). "You're only as old as you feel": Self-perception of age, fears of aging, and life satisfaction from adolescence to old age. *Psychology and Aging, 4,* 73–78.

Morgenthaler, L. (1990). A study of group processes: Who's got what floor? *Journal of Pragmatics, 14,* 537–557.

Murata, K. (1994). Intrusive or cooperative? A cross-cultural study of interruptions. *Journal of Pragmatics, 21*(4), 385–400.

Nuessel, F. H. (1982). The language of ageism. *The Gerontologist, 22*(3), 273–276.

Ochs, E. (1979). Transcription as theory. In E. Ochs & B. B. Schieffelin (Eds.), *Developmental pragmatics* (pp. 43–72). New York: Academic Press.

Paoletti, I. (1991). *Being unpopular: An analysis of a conversation with three primary school students.* Paper presented at the international conference "Current Work in Ethnomethodology and Conversational Analysis," University of Amsterdam, The Netherlands.

Paoletti, I. (1995). *The production of the foreigner child.* Paper presented at the Symposium "Writing, identity and social power in school and community context: An interactional perspective" AERA Conference, San Francisco, USA.

Paoletti, I. (1996). La construzione sociale dell'immagine dell'anziana [The social construction of the older woman's image]. *Oggidomani Anziani, IX*(1), 21–35.

Paoletti, I. (1997a). *Constructing senility: A study in the production of incoherence.* Paper presented at the international conference "Order and Disorder in Talk," UCL, London, UK.

Paoletti, I. (1997b). *Women caregivers of older people: The effect of caring in their lifestyle and health.* Research Report, INRCA, Ancona, Italy.

Paoletti, I. (1997c). La produzione dell'identià nell'intervista con anziane [Identity production in interviews with older women]. In A. Macarino (Ed.), *Analisi della Conversazione e prospettive di ricerca in Etnometodologia* [Coversational analysis and research perspectives in ethnomethodology] (pp. 235–247). Urbino: Quattroventi.

Paoletti, I., Giacalone, F., Perfetti, R., & Zuccherini, R. (1994). *L'identità sospesa* [The uncertain identity]. Firenze: Arnaud.

Paoletti, I., Sclater, E., & Kysow, J. (1993). Older women in action. *The International Journal of Community Education, 1*(4), 25–28.

Peretz, S., & Soeur, R. (Eds.). (1996). *Older women's network, Europe.* Draft Constitution, Munster.

Rubin, A. M., & Rubin, R. B. (1986). Contestual age as a life position index. *International Journal of Ageing and Human Development, 23*(1), 27–45.

Sacks, H. (1972). On the analyzability of stories by children. In J. J. Gumperz & D. Hymes (Eds.), *Directions in sociolinguistics: The ethnography of communication* (pp. 216–232). New York: Holt, Rinehart & Winston.

Sacks, H. (1992). *Lectures on conversation* (Vols. 1 & 2). Oxford, England: Blackwell.

Schegloff, E. (1988). Description in the social sciences: Talk-in-interaction. *IPrA Papers in Pragmatics*, 2(1–2), 1–24.

Schenkein, J. (1978). Identity negotiation in conversation. In J. Schenkein (Ed.), *Studies in the organization of conversational interaction* (pp. 57–77). New York: Academic.

Segatori, R., Benvenuti, P., & Gristina, D. A. (1989). *Disagio psichico, salute della donna e terza età: Lo stato dei servizi in Umbria negli ultimi 20 anni* [Women's psychological problems, health and third age: The services in Umbria in the last 20 years]. Napoli: Edizioni Scientifiche Italiane.

Shotter, J., & Gergen, K. J. (1989). *Texts of identity*. London: Sage.

Silverman, D. (1987). Constituting the subject, In: *Communication and medical practice* (pp. 134–190). Newbury Park: Sage.

Silverman, D. (1993). *Interpreting qualitative data*. London: Sage.

Smith, D. E. (1990). The social organization of subjectivity: An analysis of the micro-politics of a meeting. In *Text, facts & femininity* (pp. 53–85). London: Routledge.

Spender, D. (1980). *Man made language*. London: Routledge & Kegan.

Stolnitz, G. J. (Ed.). (1994). Social aspects and country reviews of population aging. Europe and North America. *Economic Studies* n. 6, New York: United Nations.

Taylor, B. (1992). Elderly identity in conversation. Producing frailty. *Communication Research*, 19(4), 493–515.

ten Have, P. (1994). *Formatting the consultation: Communication format and constituted identities*. Paper presented at the Sociolinguistic Session of the 13th World Congress of Sociology, Bielefeld, Germany.

Uhlenberg, P. (1992). Population aging and social policy. *Annual Review of Sociology, 18*, 449–474.

Watson, D. R., & Weinberg, T. S. (1982). Interviews and the interactional construction of accounts of homosexual identity. *Social Analysis, 11*, 56–78.

Watson, R. (1987). Interdisciplinary considerations in the analysis of pro-terms. In G. Button & R. E. Lee (Eds.), *Talk and social organization* (pp. 261–289). Clevedon: Multilingual Matters Ltd.

West, C., & Zimmerman, D. H. (1985). Gender, language, and discourse. In T. A. van Dijk (Ed.), *Handbook of discourse analysis* (Vol. 4, 103–124). London: Academic.

Wilson, T. P. (1991). Social structures and the sequential organization of interaction. In D. Boden & D. H. Zimmerman. *Talk and social structure* (pp. 22–43). Cambridge, UK: Polity.

Author Index

Subject Index